Fernandina Beach

Tallahassee

Jacksonville

St. Augustine

Gainesville

Daytona Beach

ATLANTIC OCEAN

Orlando

CAPE KENNEDY

Lakeland

Tampa

St. Petersburg

Ft. Pierce

Sarasota

Lake Okeechobee

West Palm Beach

THE EVERGLADES

EVERGLADES NATIONAL PARK

Fort Lauderdale

Miami Beach

Hialeah

Miami

IDA

FLORIDA BAY

DRY TORTUGAS

Key West

STRAITS OF FLORIDA

art work: Ladislav Hennel

FLORIDA *A Place In The Sun*

FLORIDA

A Place In The Sun

Photographs by Heinz Erhardt
Text by Al Burt

Published by Burda GmbH

"The question of
Florida is a question of an
indefinite enlargement
of many people's pleasures
and of many people's
existences as against that
universal killing ague
of modern life... Here one
has an instinct that it
is one's duty to repose broad-
faced upward, like fields
in the fall, and to lie fallow
under suns and airs..."

— — poet Sidney Lanier, introducing his guidebook
(Florida: Its Scenery, Climate, and History), 1875.

Publisher:

DR. FRANZ BURDA

Supervising Editor:
Claus Preute

Layout:
Heinz Roßkopf

Chief of Production:
Heinz Morstadt

Layout-Assistance:
Horst Prestenbach
Karl-Heinz Steuer

Production-Assistance:
Armin Wendlandt
Heinz Vetter

© 1974 by BURDA GMBH,
Offenburg
Printed in West Germany

Library of Congress Catalog
Card Number: 74-84000
International Standard Book
Number (ISBN): 0-914962-00-0

Distributed in Florida:
by The Florida Chamber
of Commerce, 311 South Calhoun
Street, P. O. Box 5497
Tallahassee, Florida 32301

Distributed to bookstores
outside of Florida:
by Dietz Press
109 East Cary Street
Richmond, Virginia 23219

Contents

A Unique Place

Florida hangs off the southeastern United States like a pendant, outlined in sandy white beaches, jewelled with 30,000 lakes and beribboned with 1,711 streams. It has splendor and mystery. Great swamps splash it dark and green, and 17 powerfully bubbling springs make it sparkle. Yet that is only the body of Florida. Its soul derives from the sun.

Florida has a flat top, called the Panhandle, that begins in the shadow of Alabama near Pensacola. It moves east in a narrow strip that skinnies out over the Gulf of Mexico. Then a long, fat finger forms, jointed to Georgia and surrounded on the other sides by the ocean. It points toward the Caribbean and runs 400 miles south to Miami. From Pensacola to Miami is a 700-mile drive and there is more Florida yet. A 150-mile string of islands, called the Keys, curl off that finger like waterdrops in an ocean breeze. At the end is Key West. After God made Florida, a favorite story goes, he threw the scraps out to sea. They became the Keys.

Over all this the sun presides with varying degrees of attention. In the South, generally, winter hardly comes at all. In central Florida, it visits just a little more. In north Florida and the Panhandle, freezing days fill an average of less than three weeks each year. The temperature difference between north and south during those relatively cool months hovers around 13 degrees. So there is variety under the sun, too. You can stay warm all winter, enjoy the exhilarating nip of occasional frost or experience the change of seasons. Florida handles it all quite nicely.

The Gulf Stream must get credit, too. That powerful stream, which flows through oceans rather than land, washes the southern tip of Florida with 100 billion tons of warm water every hour. It curves around the finger at a speed of four knots and moves up the east coast. Seamen historically have ridden its current to advantage. If no one fully can explain the mystery of the Gulf Stream, few Floridians question its blessings.

The coastline from Pensacola around to Fernandina Beach at the northeast corner makes a broad sweep of 1,300 miles, more than any other state except Alaska. Speckled along the coasts are the islands and inlets once used as pirate lairs, and most of the people. The water, both coastal and inland, draws people hypnotically, and it is everywhere. There may be no other state with so many fishermen and boaters, for not only is Florida bounded on three sides by the oceans, but 4,308 square miles (from a total 58,560) of the peninsula itself are

water. Geologists explain that Florida's mostly sandy soils cover a subsurface of clay or layers of limestone. Under certain conditions, over a long period of time, the limestone rock dissolves. When it does, a sinkhole appears. These sinkholes and depressions, filled by rainwater or springs, account geologically for the state's superb system of fresh-water lakes and connecting streams and canals so inviting to sportsmen. Since no place in Florida is more than 60 miles from tidal water, the fisherman's choice is convenient as well as broad. The longest river, the St. Johns, flows 273 miles out of central Florida in a winding course northward to the Atlantic Ocean east of Jacksonville. The most famous river, the Suwannee, rises out of south Georgia's Okefenokee Swamp and meanders 177 miles across the state past stands of tall cypress trees, through eroded limestone banks and along palm-lined sandy bluffs to the Gulf of Mexico midway between the capital Tallahassee and Tampa.

Along a high, wide ridge that runs through the center of the state, the famed Florida oranges grow among rolling hills. As the land flattens, cattle ranches appear. Near the west coast, phosphate mines show. Farther north and east, between the lake country and the Atlantic Ocean, potatoes and cabbage decorate the fields and there are more ranches. In the south around the 730-square-mile Lake Okeechobee, sugar cane and vegetables pop up out of the black earth. Below the 1.4 million acre Everglades National Park, more winter vegetable crops compete for land southwest of Miami with housing for a population that forever seems to be doubling itself. In the north, through the Panhandle, the highlands reappear. At the little town of Lakewood, near the Alabama border, Florida's highest hill reaches to an elevation of 345 feet. Forests feed the pulpmills. Plowed fields sprout tobacco, soybeans, peanuts and corn. In the far northwest, oil derricks rise out of rural pastures near the town of Jay.

Florida's vegetation and wildlife vary with the climate that ranges from temperate in the north to tropical in the south. Varieties of palm, pine, oak and cypress trees grow over most of the state, frequently with the graceful, grey Spanish moss hanging from their limbs. Palmetto clumps are frequent. Sea oats and other grasses help anchor the undeveloped dunes. Mangroves line the coastal marshes of the south, where the more exotic flowers, shrubs and fruit trees are numerous. The fish and other marine life vary, too, with salt water offering almost limitless variety, and freshwater tempting sportsmen with a range of catch from the small bream to the world famous black bass. Around the more remote swamps and streams, particularly in the parks and refuges, alligators and turtles remain numerous. Over much of the state, depending upon the press of population, can be found deer, rabbit, squirrel, raccoon, armadillo, opossum, fox, bobcat, turkey and quail, as well as an occasional bear and panther. The most spectacular look at nature, however, for many comes in the millions of migrating and native birds. Bird lovers find it a paradise. There may be no other state with more rare species. Among those that excite the birdwatchers are the bald eagle, flamingo, roseate spoonbill, common brown pelican, the many herons, egrets and cranes.

This wonderfully complex state, which explorers in the early 16th century found both dangerous and irresistible, ranks among the U. S. top tier in population. About 1880, after the Civil War and Reconstruction, the wealthy began to sample the winter sun and stayed to pioneer development. That year, the census showed Florida with a population of 270,000. Twenty years later, it had doubled. In another 20 years, it almost had doubled again. Population leaped forward in the Boom period of the 1920's, slowed during the 1930's Depression, but by 1940 numbered just under 2 million residents and was growing again. After World War II, the population took off, like one of Cape Canaveral's rockets, nearly doubling between 1950 and 1960 to 5.2 million persons. As Florida became the playground of all, and not just the wealthy, tourism kept pace. In 1950, 4.7 million tourists came to Florida. Two decades later, with a population of 7 million and still growing, tourism had climbed over the 23 million mark annually.

Each tourist became a potential new resident. Statisticians estimated in the 1970's that Florida welcomed up to 7,000 new permanent residents a week and, looking to years ahead, they foresaw no end to it. In less than 100 years, Florida remarkably had been transformed from wilderness to an eagerly sought place in the sun.

While Pensacola and St. Augustine were the first sites where Spanish explorers tried to found settlements, development first centered on such areas as Jacksonville and Tampa, later to the Palm Beaches, Fort Lauderdale and Miami and the tropical south, and finally spread again back upstate to include the beautiful southwest coast around Naples and Fort Myers, and the middle area of Orlando.

Tallahassee boomed, too. It has been said that Florida filled like a bottle, from the bottom up. Yet there remained large gaps of nature, some in the Panhandle and the north simply not yet reached by development and others protected by national forests and parks and wildlife refuges. Huge tracts devoted to timber and citrus and cattle assured the survival of green spaces to contrast with the great cities.

Florida, the southernmost state, became in the process the least southern in lifestyle, though it retained a tendency toward political conservatism. Along the Panhandle and in the gracious city of Tallahassee, as well as some other sections of north Florida, a sense of the U. S. South was cherished and it survived. Elsewhere, migration made the state too cosmopolitan for regional identity. The original tourists, wealthy Swells from the U. S. North, were overrun by the great in-migration that followed them. From all over the United States, new customs and accents and attitudes mixed and blended with those already here, and in turn with those that followed. The Crackers, a nickname for rural Floridians, retreated as the wildlife did before population pressures. Their survivors, and those of the Swells at the other end of the economic pole, moderated their individualistic customs as Florida grew up.

A favorite story in Florida legend tells of an encounter in the late 19th century between a Cracker boy and a Yankee Swell who looked upon the lad as primitive. "What do you live on in Florida?" the Swell inquired of the little Cracker. The boy replied, "Alligators and cabbage palm in the summer time, and sick Yankees in the winter."

The Crackers and Swells, however, long ago became minorities in Florida. In fact, nearly everyone in Florida belongs to a minority of one kind or another. Among the more distinct of these are the elderly retirees, who come to Florida in great numbers; Cuban political refugees, who settled principally in Miami's "Little Havana" and Tampa's Ybor City; the Seminole Indians, the only legitimate natives; the wellknown Greek colony of fishermen around Tarpon Springs; the Czechoslovakian village of Masaryktown just north of Tampa, and the Conchs (descendants of Bahamians) throughout the Keys.

All of this fills, in the fashion of a Christmas stocking, the fat U. S. finger that points toward Cuba. Each visitor, and each resident, can seek and find something special within its infinite variety. But for all, it has the certain magic of a place in the sun.

9

The Miracle Strip, a summertime playground for Florida's Panhandle, begins here at Panama City and stretches to Pens

ola. Clear waters, gently rolling surf and the powdery white beaches combine to make it one of the state's most popular

Dozens of fishermen jam these rails of a concrete pier north of Miami Beach, peering from under sun hats, chomping on ci

...rs or cigarets and bristling with rods and reels as they wait anxiously for some courageous fish to run their seaside gauntlet

13

From the air, Miami's finely meshed expressway system looks like a tangled skein of concrete ribbon which makes a pack[...]

ge of the entire city. The skyline bursts upward in the distance to mark a boulevard where it runs parallel to Biscayne Bay.

In a blaze of early morning light, a solitary, determined fisherman wades out into the shallow waters of Tampa Bay ne

r St. Petersburg's Sunshine Skyway for some surf-casting at an hour when there are no competitors except the fish.

The Way It Was

For perhaps 10,000 years, men have found reasons and ways to come to Florida. The first probably walked across from Asia on a skinny ridge of land that touched Alaska, and followed a path south until they found a warm place.

These were Indians, and they had Florida all to themselves until early in the 16th century. By then, the Spanish explorer Columbus had set Europe afire with romantic stories of the New World he discovered in 1492. The ambitious and the adventuresome on the continent, especially in Spain, were feverish to follow.

Juan Ponce de Leon, another Spaniard, officially reached Florida before the other Europeans. Others probably preceded him but history credits Ponce de Leon because he left the best records. He had joined Columbus' second voyage in 1493 to the Caribbean Island of Hispaniola, had accumulated wealth after the king appointed him governor of neighboring Puerto Rico and hungered for more.

Ponce de Leon returned to Spain and petitioned the king for a patent to discover and govern islands to the north, in particular the fabled island of Bimini, where not only riches but the legendary Fountain of Youth supposedly waited. The king granted permission and Ponce de Leon, more than 50 years old, set sail March 3, 1513, from Puerto Rico in three small ships — the Santa Maria de Consolaciòn, the Santiago and the San Cristobal de San Juan. While youthful rejuvenation undoubtedly interested him, visions of gold and slaves and power fascinated the practical Ponce even more.

About four weeks later, April 2 of the Easter season, his ships landed on the Florida coast, probably just north of St. Augustine, and Ponce de Leon went ashore to plant the Spanish flag. It was not Bimini, but the springtime beauty of the land so impressed him that he called it La Florida, after the Eeast of Flowers.

Though he found Indian hostility rather than gold, Ponce de Leon remained convinced that the Florida wilderness hid vast treasures. He sailed along the east coast, around the Keys and explored harbors up the gulf coast. He went back to Puerto Rico in September, determined to return.

The Indians were spread throughout Florida, with each tribe an empire. In southern Florida, there were nomadic, warlike hunters and fishermen — including tribes of the Calusas, the Tequestas and the Ais. In northern Florida, a more settled and developed Indian society included the Apalachees and the Timucuas.

Ponce de Leon came back in 1521 with another charge from the king, this time to conquer, colonize and govern Florida. He chose the gulf coast, brought with him priests and the authority to enslave those Indians who would not be converted to Christianity. As the colonists built houses and shelters, the Calusas attacked and drove them back to their ships. An Indian arrow wounded Ponce de Leon. He was able to reach Cuba before dying.

For him, and many other fortune-hunters during the next four centuries, Florida meant disappointment and tragedy. Its treasures were not of coin, and not really understood or appreciated by any but the Indians for nearly four centuries.

Whatever his fate, the Ponce de Leon mission renewed the fever in Europe. In South America and Mexico, Spanish explorers had found advanced Indian civilizations and immense stores of precious metals. Florida was regarded as an untapped source in that same wealthy New World.

One after another, for the next half-century, Spaniards blazed their way into Florida, failed, and died. The complex peninsula literally swallowed them. In 1528 Panfilo de Narvaez sailed with four ships from Cuba and landed near Tampa Bay. Fired by Indian stories of gold, he went inland. Eight years later, four survivors reached Mexico City with horror stories that fascinated all but deterred few.

The Spanish explorer first touched Florida in 1539, near the present city of Bradenton, mistakenly expecting to find gold and treasure. Each year, a costumed festival re-creates that historic event in a happier frame. Rather than Indians, hostility and hardship, the modern DeSoto encounters happy crowds, yachts and parties.

Bradenton festival depicts arrival of Hernando DeSoto

Out of the Narvaez expedition came one of Florida's most romantic Indian stories, told in The Wilderness Tattoo by William O. Steele. The Timucuas captured Juan Ortiz, a 17-year-old Spanish lad who had been with Narvaez. They tortured and killed his three companions, and tied Juan across a lattice-work of green sticks above the banked coals of a pit fire. He would have roasted alive had not the Timucua chief's wife and daughter intervened. The women nursed him back to health and helped him escape to a neighboring tribe, where he lived happily if strangely until Hernando DeSoto came to Florida in 1539.

DeSoto, wealthy and famous for his part in the conquest of Peru, arrived at Tampa Bay with a fleet of 10 vessels and the largest expedition yet. He had soldiers, priests and workers as well as pigs, cattle and dogs. When Juan Ortiz came to him, appearing more Indian than Spaniard, DeSoto enlisted him as interpreter and guide, and moved northward into Apalachee country. Battling the Indians as well as the wilderness, it took him nearly three years to chase the stories of gold and treasure still farther north and west to the Mississippi River. In A History of Florida, by Charlton Tebeau, DeSoto's path is traced through Georgia into the Carolinas and finally west across Alabama to the river. There, like the others, he died.

DeSoto's experience, and other failures that followed in the next 17 years, took the glow off Florida. The Spanish began to despair either of finding great wealth, a livable area for colonizing or an Indian society they could convert or enslave. Still, the king needed a colony to establish Spanish claim to the land, to protect or furnish way stations for Spanish ships, and as additional defense for Spanish claims in Mexico and South America. The next Spanish attempt came in 1559 at Pensacola Bay under the leadership of Tristan de Luna, an early associate of DeSoto. Storms, scarcities of food and resulting ill health, plus grumbling over De Luna's leadership finished the colony in two years. After 50 years of trying, Spain still had no base in Florida.

The Spanish finally succeeded because of the French. For some time, both France and England had been envious of the great wealth Spain was draining out of the New World, but they dared not interfere. When the Tristan de Luna mission failed, making Spanish discouragement over Florida evident, the French took a hand. Not only did Florida offer the promise of new lands and power for France, but a safety valve for fierce religious conflicts between Catholics and Huguenots (Protestants) at home.

In 1562, Jean Ribault, a Huguenot and France's most famous sea captain, commanded a three-ship expedition to explore Florida as a site for a Huguenot colony. He reached the mouth of the St. Johns River April 30, 1562, sailed inland for about five miles, and anchored at a broad bluff along the south bank of the river. What he saw enchanted him.

"The fairest, frutefullest and pleasantest of all the worlds," wrote Ribault. "The sight of the faire-meadows is a pleasure not able to be expressed with tongue." His second-in-command, Rene Laudonniere, bubbled as well. "The place was so pleasant that melancholias would be forced to change their nature," he commented later.

In honor of the date, they called it the River of May, and sailed home with notebooks full, planning to gather colonists and return to found a permanent settlement.

The French did not make it back until 1564, and then under the command of Laudonniere. Stymied at home because of the religious war, Ribault went to England seeking help, and was imprisoned. Before he could be released, the situation in France eased and in 1564, three French ships under Laudonniere's command returned to the broad bluff on the River of May.

Laudonniere brought 300 men and four women, nearly all of them Huguenots, erected a triangular fort of earth and wood and named it Fort Caroline, after French King Charles IX. The French made friends with the Timucuas, fermented wine and learned to smoke tobacco. For awhile, the prospects appeared good.

But they let themselves become too dependent upon the Indians for food, and when a quarrel broke out among the tribes, it also involved the French and restricted their food supply. While Laudonniere sought to strengthen the fort, and hold any treasures found for the king, the men chafed at the shortages of food, the restraints on seeking gold, and Laudonniere's moralistic views on Indian maidens. Charles E. Bennett rendered details of this settlement in his book titled, Laudonniere and Fort Caroline.

Two mutinies occurred. Each time, the mutineers stole vessels and took to the seas to plunder Spanish treasure ships, whose route followed the Gulf Stream current up the Florida coast past Fort Caroline and then toward the Azores and home. All this stung the Spanish into action. The French were tampering with the flow of gold from the New World colonies.

The Spanish reacted in 1565 by putting an armada of 19 ships under the command of Pedro Menendez de Aviles, their foremost admiral.

The king ordered him to oust the French, establish permanent Spanish settlements on the coast and convert the Indians into Christians and allies. Meanwhile, Jean Ribault, out of the French prison, sailed from France with reinforcements for the troubled Fort Caroline.

The two commanders raced to reach there first, and Ribault won the race. He arrived just as the Huguenots were preparing to abandon the fort. Menendez ran into storms that reduced his fleet and he put into Puerto Rico. He put out to sea again with less than half his original fleet, making the French now the superior force.

Conqueror: with sword, plumed hat and cape

While DeSoto may have dreamed of conquering new worlds for Spain, he did not dress properly for an attentive Florida sun. Any tourist these days could tell him to forget the heavy stuff but be sure to pack shorts and swim trunks, sunglasses and suntan lotion. And he ought to swap that sword for a rod and reel.

The drums roll, the
cannons boom and tourists hang
off the old fort wall
to watch history come alive

In St. Augustine, the city named and created by Pedro Menendez, the Spanish influence remains dominant historically. Although the British once held the city, changing the name of the Castillo to Fort Marion, they could erase neither its Spanish soul nor face. Annual celebrations reflect this. Here, the U.S. flag flutters in the breeze off Matanzas Bay as Spanish troopers gather for assembly.

Menendez followed the Florida coast to a harbor 40 miles south of the St. Johns River, anchored, and celebrated the feast day of Saint Augustine with High Mass. He gave the place that name. Menendez then proceeded to the St. Johns to survey the enemy. A brief encounter with four French ships settled nothing, except to alert them, and Menendez hurried back to St. Augustine to await an attack. Sept. 8, 1565, his men went ashore in St. Augustine and on that date it officially became the first permanent settlement by Europeans in Florida.

Ribault, against Laudonniere's advice, decided to attack the Spanish, just as Menendez expected. Ribault took most of the ablebodied men from Fort Caroline and sailed toward St. Augustine. Had it not been low tide, Ribault might have captured Menendez in the harbor, but Ribault's heavier ships could not cross a sandbar guarding the entrance. While they waited for high tide, a hurricane hit, driving the French ships south and wrecking them on the beaches.

Menendez, ever bold, guessed the situation at Fort Caroline and made an incredible march through swamps, rivers and wilderness to reach there in four days. Taken by surprise, the French had no chance. Within an hour, the men were dead and the women and children captives. Those soldiers not killed in battle were hanged beneath a placard that read, "I do this, not as to Frenchmen, but as to Lutherans (Huguenots)." Laudonniere was among the few who escaped.

Word reached Menendez that 200 or more of Ribault's shipwrecked men were marching north. With 50 men, the Spaniard hurried to intercept them at an inlet 15 miles south of St. Augustine. In response to Menendez' promises to give them God's mercy, the battered, hungry Frenchmen surrendered. After binding their hands behind them, Menendez killed all except the few who were Catholics. The inlet was named to memorialize that day. It is called Matanzas, the Spanish word for slaughter.

The incredible sequence of events was not over yet. In France, there was an uproar. But Spain argued the men were pirates, and heretics as well. To prevent an open break, nothing officially was done. However, a 40-year-old distinguished French Catholic, Dominique de Gourgues, put together a force which he said was for slave trade, and sailed toward Florida in 1568, while Menendez was in Spain.

De Gourgues caught Fort Caroline, then called San Mateo, by surprise. With 180 men, he burned the fort, killed or captured those inside. He hanged the captives beneath a vengeful placard, "Not as to Spaniards, but as to Traitors, Robbers and Murderers."

France had its revenge, and that ended the first international conflict among Europeans for territory that was to become the United States. It also dulled the French appetite for Florida.

Menendez lived for another seven years, dying in Spain during another visit there." After the salvation

of my soul," he wrote a few weeks before his death, "There is nothing in this world I want more than to be in Florida, saving souls." A sympathetic account of Menendez' life was written by Albert Manucy, called Florida's Menendez.

Once the French were defeated, Menendez' task had been to sweep the seas free of pirates, and to secure Florida for Spain with a combination of military posts, settlements and missions. Florida then, to the Spanish, included most of what is now the United States, though their knowledge of it for the most part included only the peninsula itself, areas along the Atlantic coast as far north as Chesapeake Bay, west along the Gulf coast around the bend and down to Mexico.

The Menendez settlements included Santa Elena (Port Royal, S. C.), St. Augustine, Santa Lucia (near Cape Canaveral), San Anton (Charlotte Harbor), Tocobago (Tampa Bay), and Tequesta (Miami). St. Augustine was his principal survivor. Spain learned from the Menendez efforts that the old dreams for Florida were wrong. It would yield neither enough wealth, nor slaves, nor other trade to make it a profitable colony in the style of Peru and Mexico. Its importance was strategic.

As a chain of Spanish missions grew across Florida, stretching west into the Apalachee country as well as north, so did troubles between Spain and England. English adventurers began to loot the treasure-laden Spanish galleons as they headed home. Though the Queen officially disapproved, privately they were encouraged. War for control of the seas, and therefore the New World, became inevitable.

In 1586, after a marauding tour of Spanish ports to the south, Sir Francis Drake raided and burned the St. Augustine fort, then built of timber. Spain reacted to the challenge by putting together a Great Armada, and sending it against England in 1588. Defeat of the armada, following the jolt of Drake's raid, seriously shook Spain's grip. The English followed up by establishing a series of settlements, including one at Jamestown, Virginia, in 1607, and continued harassment. Those, together with Indian hostility, began to push the Spanish out of the upper reaches of Florida and back toward the peninsula itself. The English appeared to recognize the Indians had rights, and managed better relations with them. In 1670, after England had moved as far south as Charleston, S. C., the weakened Spanish attempted to appease her with a treaty that recognized English authority from Charleston north. This, the Spanish hoped, would stop them. It did not. They continued to come south. To make matters worse, the French began encroaching from the north and west, coming down the Mississippi River to its mouth.

Spain decided to fight. First, it had to build a more substantial fort at St. Augustine, which the English regularly sacked and burned. Nine wooden forts had been destroyed. The Spanish in 1672 began cons-

truction of the Castillo de San Marcos, made of coquina, a stone formed from a mixture of sand and shells. It took 30 years for the fort to take enough shape to afford a defense, but the heart of Spanish Florida finally was protected. In addition, the string of Spanish missions across Florida was drawn into the military defense and the luckless Indian converts recruited as allies.

All sides in the international conflict used the Indians, both to help fight the enemy, to work and to supply food, and in the slave trade. Before it was over, a combination of the wars and disease wiped out nearly all. These few later were joined by fugitives or dissidents of the Creek Indian Confederation from Alabama and Georgia, and Yamassees from South Carolina, to form an Indian amalgam that became known as the Seminoles, or "wild ones."

The Spaniards briefly went on offense, sending a raiding party from St. Augustine against Port Royal (Hilton Head), South Carolina in 1686 and, wary of the French, in 1698 re-established a fort at Pensacola Bay, calling it San Carlos. Within 166 years, the flags of five nations would fly over the settlement.

When James Moore became governor of the English colony in South Carolina in 1700, another attack was mounted on St. Augustine, the first against the new fort. Moore, fearful of an alliance between France and Spain that would endanger the colonies, and pressured by Carolinians angered by the Port Royal raid and because Spanish Florida was a haven for runaway slaves, thought he could eliminate St. Augustine.

Moore attacked by sea, his lieutenant by land, and they encountered no opposition in the settlement. Everyone had fled inside the walls of the fort. He laid seige for three months, but gave up when Spanish reinforcements arrived from Havana. Two years later, he led another force through the Apalachee country, destroying Spanish missions and Indian settlements. In the next few years, similar raids by other Englishmen succeeded in eliminating the chain of missions.

During a two-year period beginning in 1719, the fortunes of Pensacola illustrated the shifting international alliances and how they reflected in the battle for control of Florida. Twice, Pensacola was exchanged between the French and the Spanish.

Austria, Holland, France and England declared the Quadruple Alliance War against Spain. When the French settlement at New Orleans heard of the war in May, it attacked and captured Pensacola. The French had agreed to transport prisoners to Havana, but Spanish authorities seized their boats on arrival, and used them to slip back into Pensacola Bay and recapture the fort. A French fleet returned in September, and the city fell a third time. When the five nations signed a peace treaty in 1721, the terms called for Pen-

The Old City remembers the struggle

The ancient Spanish fort, Castillo de San Marcos, anchored the first European settlement to survive in Florida. Each year, St. Augustine relives its rich history in pageantry enhanced by a section where the streets and shops are just as they were when the Spanish ruled.

28

No supermarkets and shopping centers awaited the housewives in the old days at St. Augustine. When they went to the store, they encountered something that looked like this scene in the "oldest store". There was oil for the lamps (a relatively modern convenience compared to making candles from tallow), oats and corn meal and dyes and perhaps a jugful of spirits from the barrels. And no frozen food counter, either. At right, a horse trots past the store, pulling one of the tour buggies.

The way it was for shoppers

29

sacola to be returned to the control of the Spanish.

The territory from the Carolinas to Florida had become a buffer between the Spanish and British. Both contested it. But in 1733, the English king granted General James Edward Oglethorpe the rights of colonization. The action opened up a new round of hostilities, and Florida bounced back and forth between Spain and England for nearly a century before finally and permanently going to the new nation, the United States, in 1821.

Since neither Oglethorpe nor the Spanish, under Gov. Jose Simeon Sanchez of St. Augustine, were really prepared for war, the Spanish suggested negotiation. Sanchez agreed to the St. Johns River as a dividing line. In Spain, his superiors were so infuriated at this backward step that they called him home, where he was executed. The war resumed.

When the English declared The War of Jenkins' Ear against Spain in 1739 (fought over an English smuggler who claimed the Spanish had caught his vessel and trimmed off his ear), Oglethorpe moved within a year. From January to July, he tried to take the fort at St. Augustine and failed. When heavy Spanish warships arrived as reinforcements, he gave it up and went back to Georgia.

The Spanish struck back, loosing their privateers against English coastal plantations and at one point in 1742 driving overland as far north as St. Simons Island, where they lost The Battle of the Bloody Marsh and withdrew to St. Augustine. Oglethorpe attacked St. Augustine again the same year, and again was driven back.

The coquina fortress, the Castillo de San Marcos, still had not been breached but after more than two centuries, the Spanish had little else but a struggling fort and village at Pensacola to show for their efforts. The Seminole Indians had more land, and the French and British had as much or more influence.

Considering what little control the Spanish had, perhaps they did not give up so much in the Treaty of Paris in 1763. That came as the settlement of The Seven Years' War between the English and French, the climax to their long struggle for colonial supremacy. Late in the game, too late, the Spanish had joined the French in a losing cause. For its reward, England took Canada from the French and exchanged Havana, captured in the war, for Florida. To Spain, for reasons of strategy as well as pride, it was a bitter development, even though France gave her Louisiana.

The English reorganized their new territory into East Florida and West Florida. East Florida, with St. Augustine as the capital, reached to the banks of the Apalachicola River. West Florida began on the other bank and extended to the Mississippi River, with Pensacola the capital.

As they had in the 13 American colonies to the north, British rule emphasized settlement and friendly relations with the Indians. The push south had spilled over from the Carolinas, and into Georgia, and now flowed to Florida in earnest. In the 20 years of British rule from 1763 to 1783, Florida was changed irrevocably. The English took up huge tracts for plantations, manned by slaves, and producing indigo, rice, forestry products and citrus. Land and even financial assistance were offered to those who would settle.

One of the earliest promotional pamphlets on Florida real estate came from the English, and was in circulation long before the territory even belonged to them. It talked of the profits that awaited settlers in Florida. "This place so desirable . . . seated in the most temperate clime, where the neighborhood of the golden light of heaven brings many advantages and his convenient distance secured them from the inconvenience of his scorching beams." The blurb called on "any younger brother whose spirit is elevated above the common sort, and yet the hard usage of our country hath not allowed suitable fortunes."

Among the first to respond to the new English control was Denys Rolle and Dr. Andrew Turnbull. Rolle made his effort on the St. Johns River near Palatka in 1765, the same year that the Kings Road was built through St. Augustine to Georgia. Turnbull, a Scottish physician, put together a unique Mediterranean colony in 1767 in a place he called New Smyrna, after his wife's home in Greece, and which was at the south end of the Kings Road. He recruited 1,500 settlers from the Mediterranean, including Italians, Greeks and Minorcans, and envisioned plantations growing indigo, oranges, figs and olives. The dream lasted nine years, broke up in dissension and political waves from the American Revolution.

During that revolution, beginning in 1775, Florida remained Loyalist and attracted refugees who felt the same way. In East Florida, there was relative security but both sides raided acreoss the border. The Loyalist defense force called itself the Florida Rangers. The biggest thrust came in 1778 when Gen. Robert Howe, with as many as 3,000 American revolutionists under his command, advanced on St. Augustine but fell back before a combination of the Rangers, sympathetic Indians, their own ineptness and the difficult conditions.

While the English were occupied with rebellion, the Spanish declared war against them in 1779 and began to move against West Florida. They took all the British settlements along the Mississippi River, including Natchez, captured Mobile the fallowing year and Pensacola in 1781. That was the end of British West Florida and even East Florida, now sandwiched between the Spanish and the United States, was placed in jeopardy.

In the peace treaties of 1783, the English recognized the independence of the United States,

Fort Clinch was built to protect Fernandina

In 1847, shortly after Florida became a state, the United States erected Fort Clinch to guard the entrance to the harbor at Fernandina Beach on Amelia Island. The fort, now a state park, was named for U.S. Gen. Duncan L. Clinch, who gained fame during the Indian wars. The fort ended the pocket rebellions of earlier years during which pirates ruled.

Henry M. Flagler, at the age of 71, married for the third time. He showered his bride with gifts, including money, jewels and this magnificent mansion in Palm Beach called Whitehall, constructed of white marble imported from Italy. The Flaglers shopped in Europe for the lavish interior furnishings. Now Whitehall is maintained as a museum so that tourists may appreciate the grand life style of this Florida pioneer.

For wife No. 3, he built a white, marble palace

acknowledged Spanish control of West Florida and ceded East Florida to them in exchange for the Bahama Islands and Gibraltar. Florida was back in Spanish hands but Spain's rule this time was briefer and even more turbulent than before.

Until 1821, Florida bordered on anarchy. Thousands of Loyalists abandoned their plantations, and Americans came down from the north to settle there. The United States and Spain argued over borders (with Spain yielding), and over runaway slaves, freebooters and marauding bands, some formed from the ranks of the old militia. The Seminoles, influenced by adventurers, became pawns used in the harassment of the Spanish. Additional pressure developed from Europe where France, after its revolution, demanded the return of Louisiana. Spain yielded again, and it was the United States' turn to worry whether the French might interfere with navigation rights on the Mississippi River. The United States tried to buy both an island at the mouth of the river to insure those rights, and Florida, from the French. It came away instead with Louisiana.

Florida still was the goal, however. A development in Europe provided the excuse. When Napoleon placed his brother upon the Spanish throne, the settlers reacted in anger and rebellion bloomed. Out of it came the Republic of West Florida, which asked to be annexed into the United States. In 1810, the U.S. Congress authorized President Madison to seize West Florida if a foreign power tried to occupy it. Some Americans called for war, hoping to take both Canada from the English and Florida from Spain before those two countries could mount a defense.

In East Florida, the United States encouraged a rebellion similar to the one in West Florida, but less successfully. Before the United States and England again went to war, in 1812, The Patriots of Amelia Island (on the northeast coast) declared themselves independent of Spain and asked the United States for protection. U.S. support wavered and the Patriots lasted but four years. The fate of Amelia Island typified what was happening in Florida. From 1812 to 1821, it flew five flags (in all, it has flown eight). After the Spanish reclaimed the island from the Patriots, a Scottish mercenary named Gregor McGregor captured the island and hoisted the Green Cross of Florida, making it a haven for pirates. The next improbable succession was by a Mexican pirate, Luis Aury, who hauled up his nation's banner. Before the United States took over, in 1821, President Monroe called the island a "festering fleshpot."

Because of Gen. Andrew Jackson, there was no such slippage in West Florida. Jackson, fresh from victory in the Creek Indian War which freed parts of Georgia and Alabama from Indian control, did not waver when the British occupied Pensacola and began drilling Indians and runaway slaves in the streets. Without waiting for orders, he stormed the city, and his momentum carried on through Mobile and into New Orleans, where he won a historic battle in 1815 after the war with the British already had ended.

But the Spanish remained in Florida and the United States' desire for the peninsula had not dimmed. Twice more, in 1818, Jackson rampaged into northwest Florida chasing and punishing Indians, and once hanging two Englishmen thought to be encouraging them. These campaigns later became known as the First Seminole War.

In 1819, Spain – no longer able to control or defend them – ceded both West and East Florida to the United States, receiving in return relief from private U.S. citizens' claims against Spain amounting to $5 million. In 1821, the treaty was formalized and the international battle for supremacy in Florida finally had ended. The Europeans withdrew, and Florida faced the new challenge of learning to live with itself.

With Florida under the U.S. flag, it looked even more attractive to settlers from the north. The complexities of the wilderness posed special problems, but two additional factors lifted those problems from the difficult to the near impossible. Both revolved around the Seminoles, who joined the remnants of the old tribes, the Timucuas and Apalachees and others, to raise the Indian population to a total estimated as high as 5,000. In the Florida of that day, it was an impressive number.

First, there were the old damage claims against the Spanish, amounting to $5 million, that the United States had assumed. The pressures of migration, and the debt, made it apparent that land would be the most convenient way to pay the claims. On the most desirable portions of that still unsettled, the Seminoles lived.

The second factor assured that the first could not be handled peacefully. Andrew Jackson, the effective but temperamental and impetuous general, entered politics as Florida's first appointed governor. President Monroe said of his appointment, "Smugglers and slave traders will hide their heads; pirates will disappear, and Seminoles cease to give trouble." But neither Jackson, nor his wife, Rachel, liked frontier Florida very much and politically it was a shotgun wedding. Jackson, whose previous exploits against the Seminoles had made him controversial, was being eased out of the military. President Monroe added to the general's displeasure by denying him patronage appointments he felt should have gone with the job. All this put the general in an irritable mood, and he showed it. When he ascended to the Presidency in 1829, he remembered. As far as he was concerned, the Seminoles had no rights.

Jackson stayed in Florida from June to October of 1821, and left. In that brief time, he did his usual efficient if abrasive job of setting up a

When Flagler travelled, the Rambler carried him in comfort

As Flagler pushed railroad tracks down Florida's east coast, he followed in his private train car, the Rambler. It had a vestibule for sight-seeing, an all-purpose sitting room panelled in oak that doubled as office, a cross-ventilated state room and bath plus a kitchen. Visitors to the Flagler Museum may tour this car and review its history pictorially.

single Florida under a civil government. Not, however, before he had clapped the outgoing Spanish governor in jail for what he considered unnecessary delay in transferring power, and not before he established laws designed to dampen the wickedness of the frontier cities, Pensacola and St. Augustine.

Faint signs of Florida's first boom probably began about the time the first legislature met at Pensacola in 1822. The entire territory was ready for plucking. In many areas, the first permanent settlements came with the establishment of military bases. A naval base at Key West in 1822, one year after John Simonton had bought the island from its Spanish-Cuban owner, brought residents rather than fishermen or pirates seeking brief haven. The same year a place called Cow Ford, where the Kings Road crossed the St. Johns River, was platted by Isaiah D. Hart and named Jacksonville in honor of the general and governor. But, as the American Guide Services book, Florida the Southernmost State (Federal Writers Project) pointed out, Jackson never visited the city. Two years later, in 1824, Fort Brooke began to stamp out the future of the Tampa Bay area.

The two major cities, Pensacola and St. Augustine, could not agree where the capital should be located. Neither considered the other a desirable location, for about 400 miles of rugged territory lay between, and neither the overland route nor the over water alternative around the Florida Keys was considered satisfactory. After the second legislature in 1823 at St. Augustine, they agreed on a compromise location in the red hills of Apalachee country, at a place known as Tallahassee.

With the capital chosen, the next logical step was a road connecting it with Pensacola and St. Augustine. The same year, 1824, the U.S. Congress authorized the building of a 640-mile road that would follow the old Spanish Trail from St. Augustine, through Picolata on the St. Johns River, across Alachua country to Tallahassee and from there west to Pensacola. A planter, John Bellamy, was given a contract for the Tallahassee-St. Augustine portion, and it became known as the Bellamy Road.

As president, Jackson's first message to the nation brought up the question of removing Indians from Florida. The issue had been growing since 1823, when the Treaty of Moultrie Creek had foreshadowed what was to come. That called for the Seminoles to be forced into reservations along Florida's sandy, north central ridge. At the time, the governor, William P. Duval, acknowledged the pressure. In Florida The Long Frontier, by Marjorie Stoneman Douglas, the governor is quoted, "The lands are wretchedly poor and cannot support them."

A year later (1830), President Jackson signed the Indian Removal Bill, which called for them to be transferred to lands in the West. That year, Florida's first federal census counted a population of 34,730. In 1832, the Treaty of Payne's Landing was signed near Silver Springs on the Oklawaha River. A Seminole delegation traveled to the Arkansas Territory to inspect the lands, and upon return (1833), signed the Treaty of Fort Gibson approving their proposed home.

Many Seminole leaders did not sign or support these treaties, and Florida moved toward violence. For more than a year, the Seminoles prepared secretly for war. During this period, a young sub-chief, Osceola, began to emerge as their most fiery spokesman and their leading military strategist. Late in December, 1835, the war began with two Indian attacks.

Osceola led one against Fort King (Ocala), killing and scalping the Indian agent Wiley Thompson and five others. On the same day, about 40 miles away, a relief column of 110 men under the command of Major Francis L. Dade was en route to Fort King from Fort Brooke. Near the site of present-day Bushnell, the Seminole chief Micanopy and his forces attacked from ambush. Dade and all but three of his men were killed. Osceola arrived in time for the victory party.

Indian attacks followed across much of the Florida frontier, and refugees poured out of the country and into the relative safety of the cities. New forts began to go up across Florida, among them Fort Dallas on the present site of Miami, Fort Pierce along the Indian River, Fort Lauderdale farther south on the east coast, Fort Harvie (later renamed Fort Myers) on the west coast at the mouth of the Caloosahatchee River, and Fort Gatlin (Orlando) in central Florida.

The year 1837 was a bad one for all concerned. The war, a couple of hard winters and a decline in cotton prices produced a financial panic. Banks and railroads, just struggling into existence, collapsed. The army, desperate for a victory over the Seminoles and their feared guerrilla strategist, Osceola, lured him to talk under a flag of truce and captured him. He died a year later in a Charleston, S.C. prison. The attending physician cut off Osceola's head, it was said, and would hang the skull on his sons' bedposts to intimidate them into good behavior.

Officially, there was no armistice. The war just faded away. In 1842, some Seminoles accepted removal to the West and most of the fighting stopped. Others went into hiding in south Florida's vast Everglades swamp, but there was occasional violence. One notable instance was the murder, in 1840, of Dr. Henry Perrine and six others at their settlement on Indian Key. Dr. Perrine had chosen this spot in the Florida Keys to conduct experiments in tropical plants and trees.

For the United States, and Florida in particular,

At this vinecovered spot the Spanish put a cross

At Mission Of Nombre De Dios, one of St. Augustine's many historical sights, the Spanish are believed to have planted a cross and established the first Christian chapel in what was to become the United States. The mission grounds include many relics of the city's rich religious heritage. Old St. Augustine has recreated the appearance of the days of Menendez.

it had been a costly war. In their book, Osceola The Unconquered Indian, William and Ellen Hartley estimated the U.S. cost at between $30 million and $40 million, plus 1,500 deaths. Seminole warriors never numbered more than 1,500, said the Hartleys, against a force that exceeded 40,000. The history of this war made Osceola a hero to all Floridians.

In 1845, Florida became the 27th state. Farms and plantations, some manned by slaves, stretched across the state from the Suwannee River to the Apalachicola River, and along the coasts and rivers south. The cattle industry grew. Steamboats moved up and down the rivers. Military outposts that had been started during the Seminole wars became the bases for new settlements, and new roads opened among them for trading. In 1850, the census showed 87,445 residents in Florida; 10 relatively peaceful years later it had jumped to 140,424. Florida was beginning to boom again. Railroads stretched from Fernandina across the state to Cedar Key on the gulf coast, and from Jacksonville to Tallahassee.

In 1846, the United States began to build one of its most unusual forts. On Garden Key in the Dry Tortuga islands 60 miles west of Key West, a multi-sided fort with walls five feet thick, built on three levels, was completed in 1851. For three centuries before, pirates and smugglers had used the Dry Tortugas, and its location appeared militarily strategic. But the United States found little use for it, except as a prison, after the Civil War and nearly 90 years after completion, it was turned over to the National Park Service.

Though Florida seceded from the Union in January, 1861, the third Southern state to do so, she remained on the fringes of the fighting for most of the four years that the Civil War lasted. Her value, rather than strategic, was as supplier for the Confederacy. Union forces, recognizing this, spent their efforts at blockading rather than invading and capturing her.

Throughout the war, the Yankees controlled the Florida coasts. From the outset, they held or captured forts at Pensacola, Key West, St. Augustine and Fernandina (Amelia Island). Additionally, they raided at will such places as Cedar Key, terminus of the railroad from Fernandina, and Apalachicola, Tampa and Jacksonville (this luckless city was occupied and abandoned four times). By the second year of the war, Florida in effect was surrounded by the Yankees except along the Georgia border on the north.

Confederate forces in Florida, with most of their fighting men sent to battlefields elsewhere, concentrated on assisting blockade runners slipping in and out of the long coast and upon preventing a Yankee invasion that could divide the state and stop the supply flow north into Georgia. This they did. Tallahassee was the only Southern ca-

pital east of the Mississippi River that did not fall in battle, and Rebel troops ate beef and pork and a variety of other scarce food items from Florida. Among these was salt, also used in the curing of meat, which was obtained by boiling seawater. Florida Under Five Flags, written by Rembert Patrick and Allen Morris, said combined Confederate government and private investment in the salt-making industry might have sailed as high as $10 million, a staggering sum in those days.

Florida defeated the Yankees twice in inland battles. The first of these did not come until February of 1864, after the North had taken Jacksonville for the fourth time and had decided to move west along the railroad toward Lake City. Confederate troops, under General Joseph Finegan, awaited them at Olustee Station, 13 miles from Lake City. According to Allen Morris' The Florida Handbook (1973–74), the battle began on an open field the morning of February 20, between two forces almost evenly matched in number (about 5,500 men) but the Yankees holding superior artillery. At the end of the day, the Yankees had been decisively defeated. They withdrew with 1,861 casualties, including 203 killed, as compared with the Confederates' 946 casualties, 93 of them dead. The Battle of Olustee was the single major engagement of the war fought in Florida.

The other engagement of interest, the Battle of Natural Bridge, took place in March, 1865, after the war was all but over. The Yankees invaded St. Marks on the gulf coast with 1,000 troops, intending to march on Tallahassee a few miles to the north. The Florida militia, bolstered by cadet volunteers from West Florida Seminary (now Florida State University), moved to meet them. They fought at natural bridge, where St. Marks River disappears underground for a short distance, and the hastily assembled defenders twice threw back assaults to win the day. In that the Union forces suffered nearly 150 casualties (21 dead) to the Floridians' 25 (three dead).

For Florida the difficult period immediately after the war, called Reconstruction, nominally ended in 1877 when George F. Drew was elected governor. But the dozen years it lasted were full of turmoil. Martial law existed from 1865 to 1868, when Republicans utilizing the advantages of the newly franchised black vote and the disenfranchisement of those who voluntarily served the Confederacy, won political control. It was a time of extremism. Northern radicals tried to punish and control the Rebels, and many Rebels in response moved to an opposite extremism out of which developed such infamous organizations as the Florida Council of the Ku Klux Klan in 1867. The polarization resulted in a ravelling of the rule of law, and both sides took advantage where they

Boy Scouts hold cannon inspection at Pensacola

Old Christ Church, built in 1832, now houses the Pensacola Historical Museum, one of the most important places to see in a tour of the city's historic Seville Square area. Pensacola, the city of five flags, includes a pleasing mixture of Spanish, French and British influence. The continental flavor survived both U.S. and Confederate rule.

More battles were fought to control Pensacola than have been fought for any other section of the U.S., Pensacolans boast. Therefore, they have more history to remember and need more memorials than most. Lee Square in the upper left picture pays tribute to the Confederate dead. At right is Plaza Ferdinand VII, named for the Spanish king, where Andrew Jackson received official title to Florida in 1821. The monument is to W.D. Chipley, who put the first railroad across the Panhandle. At lower left, The Lavalle House typifies early Gulf Coast architecture.

Monuments to memories in historic old Pensacola

40

could. Charges and countercharges of fraud and intimidation filled the campaign of 1876, in which Drew was elected, but his victory focussed Florida's attention again on the development of the state.

Among its other problems, Florida was broke. Its largest city was Key West, but there was little development elsewhere in south Florida. The federal census of 1880 showed the state with 269,493 residents. Jacksonville was beginning to blossom, but most of north Florida was agricultural, and large areas of the state still were wilderness.

When William D. Bloxham moved into the governor's chair in 1881, the state was land-rich and money-poor. Florida had an estimated 29 million acres in public lands, held by the Internal Improvement Fund. The IIF had been created in 1851 to manage those lands given Florida when it became a state. The IIF used the land to encourage the development of railroads, but the railroads failed after the war, and the state got its lands back along with a $1 million interest payment due on $14 million worth of bonds. Florida could not meet it, and Gov. Bloxham began to look around for help.

At that point, the first of the great dreamers and doers came to the rescue. He was Hamilton Disston, a wealthy young (37) Philadelphian first introduced to Florida by friends who included Henry S. Sanford, a wealthy and politically influential fellow Philadelphian who owned lands along the west bank of the St. Johns River some 100 miles south and slightly west of Jacksonville. Later, a city there would bear his name.

Sanford, anxious to see the state developed, persuaded Disston to take a plunge. With a down payment of $200,000, Disston bought 4 million acres at 25 cents an acre, saving Florida from bankruptcy. He also signed a contract with the Internal Improvement Fund under which he would get half of all "swamp and overflowed" land which he drained. He dredged in all directions around Lake Okeechobee, opening a channel to the Caloosahatchee River, freeing a waterway to the gulf at Fort Myers, and digging north from the lake up Kissimmee River.

Disston became fascinated with the rich lake mucklands as an area for farming and development, made heavy investments in steamboating as the future mainstay of Florida transportation and launched huge promotional campaigns in the north to sell off small tracts of land to farmers. He built an empire that stretched irregularly from Orlando to Lake Okeechobee to the gulf. An excellent history of Disston's experience, as well as that of other Florida pioneer promoters, is included in Charles E. Harner's book, Florida's Promoters, The Men Who Made It Big.

Disston set the pattern for the Florida Boomtime style. Others crowded into the state behind his initiative. But Disston, in spite of his immense lands and the wealth they represented, overextended himself and went broke.

While Disston may have made some wrong guesses, he had the right place. Men of greater wealth and vision took over. Among these were Henry B. Plant and Henry Morrison Flagler, both of whom had their first looks at Florida (though at different times) when they took their ailing wives on visits to Jacksonville to escape cold northern winters. Both saw Florida's future in terms of climate, and what that meant to it as a place to visit and to live. The IIF's generosity enhanced the lure of the railroad business, and they branched out into hotels and other businesses to increase the railroad traffic. Plant was there first.

After visiting Jacksonville in 1853, the Plants made their home in Augusta, Ga., where he became head of the southern division of a New York express company. When the Civil War began in 1861, splitting the company's holdings, he found enough backers to buy the southern property, which included shortline railroads and riverboat lines. The Confederacy needed him, and Plant expanded his lines through the pursuit of official services. After the war, turning to his friends in the North, he raised money to buy up the South's bankrupt railroads at bargain prices. He did well everywhere except in Florida, until Hamilton Disston showed the way. Then he moved into Florida and opened up the west coast. He hired Col. Henry S. Haines (for whom Haines City later was named), and they chose Cedar Key as the most likely base. He bought the old Cedar Key-Fernandina narrow gauge railroad, but the owners refused to sell him the station site in Cedar Key itself. So Plant went to Tampa. His workers arrived in 1883, the year Florida's first electric lights went on in Jacksonville.

For each mile of railroad built, according to the franchise of the line, Plant got thousands of acres of land from the IIF. On his Jacksonville, Tampa and Key West line, for example, he was awarded 13,480 acres for each mile. His acreage reached into the millions.

Meanwhile, he expanded the Plant Steamship Co., running from Tampa to Key West and Havana. For 30 years, refugees from Spanish Cuba had been making cigars in Key West. In 1886, the Cubans — including Vicente Martinez Ybor — moved their businesses to Tampa aboard Plant's steamships. Tampa offered Ybor 40 acres of land in the northeast part of the city for the bargain price of $4,000. He accepted, and that section became Tampa's Spanish quarter, still called Ybor City.

Before Plant arrived, Tampa had been known as a village vulnerable to yellow fever. In 1887, it struck again. A panic developed. Had Plant not

moved to stop it, Tampa might have been abandoned. He announced major development plans, including a mile-long wharf with railroad tracks to the end of it, a nearby hotel built out over the water, and another more elegant hotel (it cost him $3 million to build and furnish it) of Spanish-Moorish architecture modeled after the Alhambra Palace in Granada, Spain. This was the Tampa Bay Hotel and it put the city back on the track, Plant's track.

If Plant had a headstart, Flagler managed to catch up, and then some. A rivalry developed. Flagler had made his millions as a partner to John D. Rockefeller in Standard Oil, which they used as a lever to enter the railroad business in days before there were federal anti-trust laws.

Flagler first visited Jacksonville during the winter of 1878 with his first wife, Mary, who was ill. It was as far south as the railroad went at that time. When Mary died in 1881, a year later Flagler married, her practical nurse, Alice. They honeymooned in St. Augustine during a December when the temperature fell to 27 degrees below zero in New York. They came back the next winter, too, mixing with other wealthy refugees from the cold, and Flagler was sold on Florida. In the spring of 1885, before Henry Plant decided to build the Tampa Bay Hotel, Flagler made plans to build in St. Augustine what he felt would be the South's finest hotel, the Ponce de Leon.

If his hotel was to be the best, so must be the transportation to reach it. He bought the narrow gauge railroad that ran to Jacksonville, converted it to standard, and by the time the Ponce de Leon Hotel (costing $2.5 million) opened in 1888, his guests could ride in the style to which they were accustomed. There was still a problem, however. At Jacksonville, Flagler found it inconvenient to be ferried across the river. By 1890, he had eliminated that by building an all-steel bridge and the trains now could go all the way from St. Augustine to New York. Flagler's hotel and railroad were instant successes. They touched off a boom of land speculation.

When Henry Plant's Tampa Bay Hotel opened in 1891, he invited Flagler to the celebration. Flagler wired back, "Where the hell is Tampa Bay?" Plant replied, "Just follow the crowd." But, as successful as Plant was, he could not match the magic that Flagler performed the full length of the east coast in Florida. Until Flagler came, there were only villages. The winter vacation Swells rode the railroads to Jacksonville, and some endured the trip on to St. Augustine, but most either stayed where the tracks ended or floated down the St. Johns River aboard steamboats to such nearby resorts as Green Cove Springs. Flagler changed all that.

Success in St. Augustine opened the way. Farther south, the people clamored for him to keep coming. At first, he was only interested in hotels. The railroads were necessary to make the hotels more accessible. In 1890, he owned railroads as far south as Daytona Beach, but had been the initial builder of none. All were purchases. Gradually, though, the two enterprises became more equal and at the end the railroads perhaps were the larger of the two.

The same year, 1890, he had three hotels and a private mansion in St. Augustine, and one in Ormond Beach. His tracks ran to Daytona Beach, where they made connection with steamers going down the Halifax River. Within four years, he pushed them all the way to West Palm Beach. In 1893, the railroad reached Titusville, Cocoa, Rockledge and Eau Gallie, the Indian River country which provided oranges and pineapples to ship north. The next January they linked with Fort Pierce and a month later the railroad arrived at Lake Worth, that stretch of bay that now separates the cities of Palm Beach and West Palm Beach.

Flagler saw Palm Beach as the winter playground for the rich, and West Palm Beach as the commercial city which would supply the workers and house the untidy but necessary aspects of development. Both undoubtedly exceeded his expectations. Sidney Walter Martin, in his book, Florida's Flagler, said the workers originally were put in a community of tents and shanties called Styx on the Palm Beach side of Lake Worth. Later, Styx was moved across the lake to West Palm Beach, according to Martin, where it grew until it resembled in its roughness a Far West frontier town. The workers rowed across the lake to their jobs.

Flagler timed the completion of his railroad to Lake Worth with the completion of his newest and most ambitious hotel, the Royal Poinciana. From the time of its grand opening, in the spring of 1894, the hotel was a sellout. It had accommodations for 1,200 guests, superb service and rates that went up to $100 a day. Business was so good that Flagler immediately began to build another hotel, the Palm Beach Inn (later called The Breakers).

Here, at the Palm Beaches, the Flagler march down the coast paused and there was near panic in Miami, not yet an incorporated city, that he might come no farther (even though the state charter for that extension had been in hand since 1892). Two pioneer Miamians, both landowners, campaigned to persuade him. Mrs. Julia D. Tuttle and William B. Brickell offered land and arguments, but not until the winter of 1894–5 did they move him. One severe freeze hit that December, followed by another in February, and then Flagler listened. Crops had been ruined, the miracle of Florida smudged and many were abandoning the state. Helen Muir wrote, in Miami, U.S.A., that one year before the freezes, Florida

Old bricks, new ideas light up 'Quarter'

Just two blocks from Seville Square, where the first permanent settlement was located in Pensacola, you will find Seville Quarter. An old brick alleyway, print shop and hotel have been converted into saloons, restaurants and courtyard with atmosphere in harmony with history.

44

citrus groves had yielded 5,550,367 boxes of fruit, much of it shipped on the Flagler railroad. The year after the freeze, only 150,000 boxes were shipped. Flagler handed out free seed, hauled fertilizer free, made personal loans and sent a man to survey the damage. In Miami, Mrs. Tuttle sent the man back to Flagler with a box of fragrant orange blossoms. This time, Flagler was interested. There had been no freeze in Miami, and Flagler was convinced that such a place in the sun amounted to a piece of gold that the old Spanish pirates had missed.

Flagler's railroad, now called the Florida East Coast Railway, reached Biscayne Bay in April, 1896, and four months later the exuberant village of Miami incorporated. In January of the following year, another Flagler luxury hotel, the Royal Palm, opened where Miami River flows into the bay. Flagler passed his wand over Miami and brought in electricity, paved streets, a sewage system, helped establish schools and build churches. After another hard freeze hit Florida in 1899, with Miami again escaping, the city was on its way.

A New York court ruled Flagler's second wife hopelessly insane. In 1901, at the age of 71, he decided to remarry. As one of the most powerful men in Florida, as well as the United States, things went his way. In April, a bill making incurable insanity grounds for divorce passed the Florida House and the Florida Senate and was signed into law in less than three weeks. Flagler was granted a divorce in August and he took a 34-year-old bride within two weeks. For her wedding present, he built her a $2.5 million marble mansion in Palm Beach, still maintained as a museum.

While Flagler was sculpting a new face for the east coast, significant developments were taking place on the gulf coast and in the Panhandle. In a less grand manner than Flagler or Plant, but nevertheless effective, a Georgian named William D. Chipley opened up the Panhandle in 1883 with a railroad from Pensacola through De Funiak Springs, Orange and Marianna to the Apalachicola River, where it made connections to other cities in Florida and Georgia. Chipley was general manager of the Louisville and Nashville Railroads, and his project gave Pensacola the rail links and wharf facilities it needed to complement an excellent harbor. The town of Orange renamed itself in Chipley's honor.

Farther south, a significant discovery took place that not only boosted the possibilities for Plant but gave Florida an industry that would rank with cattle, citrus and timber in importance. In 1880, at the little town of Hawthorne in north central Florida's Alachua County, phosphate was discovered in a building stone quarry. Dr. C. A. Simmons' samples proved to be lowgrade phosphate. In 1883, he began to mine and convert it to fertilizer.

During the same period, there were other discoveries. Capt. Francis J. LeBaron, surveying a canal for the U.S. Army Engineer Corps, found river pebble phosphate along the Peace River southwest of Tampa. The river flows into the Gulf of Mexico at Charlotte Harbor. In 1883, as Plant's army of workers moved into Tampa, a government dredge started work digging a channel in the bay. In The Florida Phosphate Industry, Arch Fredric Blakey reports the dredge encountered limestone, blasted it with dynamite, and the resulting rock fragments were found to contain phosphate. By 1890, high-grade phosphate discoveries had been made in Polk, Manatee, Hillsborough and Manatee counties. A boom developed in the years 1892 to 1896 that was compared to California's gold-rush. The little town of Mulberry, in Polk County, where there had only been a sawmill before, became known as the phosphate capital of the world. Dunnellon, in Marion County, achieved world renown for its high-grade deposits and the rush of speculation that surrounded them.

Now it was Flagler's turn again to capture the attention of both Florida and the nation. In 1904, 74 years old but carried away with ambition, Flagler announced he would extend his railroad another 150 miles south of Miami. Incredibly, he would build bridges that would vault his rails across the Florida Keys and down to Key West. Everybody thought he was crazy.

Those were unusual years, though. By then the state had disposed of 18 million acres of land through the IIF (but not all to railroads). One year earlier, President Theodore Roosevelt had created the Republic of Panama in Central America and now he announced the United States would dig a canal across that isthmus linking the Atlantic and Pacific oceans.

Flagler had never stopped broadening his interests. He had bought and rebuilt the British Colonial Hotel in Nassau in the Bahama Islands, and joined Henry Plant in the Peninsula and Occidental Steamship Company operating out of Miami. He foresaw Key West as the nearest railroad link to the Panama Canal, to a free and friendly Cuba, and expected the U.S. Naval Station at Key West to be a steady customer. Everybody still thought he was crazy.

It took eight years, 30,000 men, masterful engineering and by some estimates nearly $50 million to complete the job. In January, 1912, The Extension Special pulled out of Miami with a load of celebrities, including Flagler himself making the trip in his private custommade railroad car, the Rambler. The Miami Herald suggested the Overseas Railroad was "the eighth wonder of the world." Flagler died just over a year later, after a fall on the marble steps of his Palm Beach mansion, but his miracle railroad lasted until a hurri-

Gas lights, banjos, brass rails, rusticity

From the Gay Nineties to the Roaring Twenties, Pensacola's Seville Quarter dips back into the past to create a nostalgic setting where tourists weary from walking streets in the historic district may relax and recuperate. Gas street lamps line the entrance. Rosie O'Grady's Warehouse portrays the showboat era, Lili Marlene's the days of World War I and Coppersmith's, the End of the Alley and the Seville Quarter courtyard borrow just a touch of old New Orleans.

cane wrecked it in the fall of 1935. Already hurt by the Depression, the FEC sold the railroad and its bridges to Florida for $640,000, according to Pat Parks in his book, The Railroad That Died at Sea. The state converted in into the Overseas Highway, which opened in 1938 and still remains the principal link between Key West and the mainland.

From the time of Disston, Plant and Flagler, the lure and future of Florida became plain. Men came as speculators, builders, tourists, permanent residents. The state gradually filled up, first along the coasts and then south and in the middle and in the north. The Spanish-American War introduced thousands of soldiers to a better place to live. The Swells from the North rolled down on the rails, and the farmers from Alabama and Georgia and the Carolinas trundled across the state line in wagons. World War I, with its training camps and new military bases, multiplied the effect of the Spanish-American War. World War II and the United States project to shoot men into space and land them on the moon, helped propel Florida into the upper tier of states in population.

After Flagler opened up Miami the dizziest period in Florida history, called the Boom, began. For six years, from 1920 to 1926, real estate promotions and dreams of instant wealth flooded Florida. Much of it was a pyramidding of paper profits, a trading of items at over-inflated values. A favorite story of the time was about the man who boasted of selling a $10,000 dog. Questioned, he said he swapped it for two $5,000 cats. However, some piled up astounding totals of real money, at least for awhile.

One of the most memorable of these was Carl Fisher, a half-blind man of exceptional vision who dropped out of school in the sixth grade. Fisher came to Miami in 1913 as a millionaire, and dredged up Miami Beach out of the bottom of Biscayne Bay. During his amazing splurge, Miami Beach land values leaped stratospherically. He went broke in 1932, and died in 1939.

While Fisher was glamorizing Miami Beach, George Merrick created the city of Coral Gables southwest of Miami from an area that had included his father's plantation. The plantation had been named Coral Gables, after the rock used in its buildings and after President Grover Cleveland's home, Gray Gables, in New Jersey. While Fisher dreamed of a seasonal playground for the rich, rivalling Palm Beach, Merrick wanted a substantial city of year-round homes. At one point he paid William Jennings Bryan, three times a candidate for the presidency of the United States, $100,000 a year to use his famed gift of oratory to help sell Coral Gables lots.

The hurricane of 1926, followed by a national financial collapse, wiped out both Merrick and Fisher financially. Merrick managed a modest comeback a few years later, and eventually became postmaster of Miami. He died in 1942.

There were many others, but these men symbolized the Florida Boom, just as Plant and Flagler had symbolized the beginning of Florida development. The Boom was a time of overbuilding, overselling, overpromoting and overdreaming, sometimes spiced with flim-flam. Polly Redford, in Billion Dollar Sandbar A Biography of Miami Beach, cited the example of a man arguing in court over a developer's promise. The man contended he had been promised he could "grow nuts" on the place. The developer insisted the buyer had only been told he could "go nuts" there.

The Boom was a wild, crazy time. Some developers promised anything, and delivered almost nothing. Buyers bought land without looking at it first, without knowing its exact location or condition. Some resold it the same way. But it was a tragic time for Florida because it stained the state with phoniness and gimmickery that was difficult to erase. No one ever has made a count of just how many dreamers rushed to see their new homesites, and found that they were under several feet of water or in impenetrable swamps. Buying Florida swampland became a national joke. Even so, the lure of the Florida dream was so great that the unwary for years continued to listen to the spiels of the unscrupulous and sign contracts before seeing their property and making certain it was dry, accessible and livable. To protect itself, Florida in later years made greater efforts to police such practices.

After the Depression, it seemed a long road back, but not only the beauty and climate of Florida remained, but systems of modern transportation, vigorous cities and a new generation of men arriving with new dreams for a place in the sun.

The pioneers, such as Disston, could not have dreamed the day would arrive when the concerns of Florida would not be for dredging, filling and developing, but for preserving those very same swamps and pesky mangroves and sawgrass. But that day came.

A kind of reverse pioneer exists in Florida today, and his role is an ambivalent one. While he wishes to see the state mature and grow, he does not wish this growth to make of it a different place, one that no longer fills his dream.

The great struggle in Florida is not one to conquer its nature, for men have discovered that nature to be brittle, even fragile. Under strain, it tends not to bend, but finally break. Thus, while the state is built it also must be nurtured.

Florida now understands, for the most part, that its place in the sun was a great gift. But one that requires handling with care.

In Capitol lobby the Great Seal of Florida

In the Florida Capitol at Tallahassee, a mosaic depicts the Great Seal of Florida as adopted by the Constitutions of 1868 and 1885. The seal shows an Indian woman scattering flowers, a rising sun, a tree and a steamboat in the bay. It is inscribed, THE GREAT SEAL OF FLORIDA, IN GOD WE TRUST. The 1970 State Legislature ruled the tree was a palm.

The Magical South

Florida divides into sections easily. The hard part is where to stop dividing. The South, for instance, seems a natural division. Yet within south Florida there are at least six others. Here, we will draw a line from Vero Beach on the east coast to Punta Gorda on the west and call everything below that the South.

When you speak of the magic of Florida, most people probably think first of the South, for here is where winter rarely visits; where the wealthy turned the strip from Palm Beach to Miami Beach into the world-famed Gold Coast; where the dazzling Florida Keys skip out into the ocean; where the unique Everglades cloak millions of acres in sawgrass, and a shallow river-like lake seeps through those grasses providing a home for an incredible chain of life; where the Seminole Indians finally found permanent reservations; where the islands, gentler surf and slower public appreciation gave the lower west coast a more deliberate character in contrast with the Gold Coast; where huge, diked Lake Okeechobee and a network of drainage canals permit vegetable farms and fields of sugarcane.

Most Floridians live in the South. To the newcomer, the sudden rains and swift return to sunshine, the rapidly growing greenery, spring-like winters, sparkling waters and long stretches of beaches give life an unreal, fairyland quality. Almost everybody came from somewhere else, and often the trip was recent. New Jersey, or Ohio, or Georgia was never like this. The landscape is so flat, the air so heavy, the moon hangs so full and low, cities are so bright with pastel and white buildings, and natives so daringly casual. Lifestyle revolves around the outdoors, around golf and tennis and swimming and fishing and boating. The homes open up and bring the lawns and gardens and swimming pools inside. After living in south Florida, existence in the colder climes of the U.S. North seems narrow and cramped. This certain quality, a kind of enchantment, explains why Forida stayed generally on a Boom incline (despite interruptions of the Depression) once modern transportation made it accessible. Old-timers used to say, "Once you get sand in your shoes, you can't stay away. You'll be back." They did come back, by the millions, each seeking his own dreams for a special place in the sun. Out of those dreams sprang the cities.

The wide, palm-lined streets of Vero Beach sit along both sides of the Indian River in the heart of one of Florida's most wellknown citrus areas. They draw a share of the winter Swells as well as the permanent population boom. Vero is one of the Florida cities that serves as the training home of a major league baseball organization. The teams play each other in a series of games each spring which are called the Grapefruit League competition. The Los Angeles Dodger organization has been part of the scene at Vero Beach since 1948. It is a point of pride for Florida that California teams trains here.

The stretch of coast from Vero Beach south past Fort Pierce and Stuart to Palm Beach never earned the renown of the Gold Coast, but its natural attractions were approximately the same. Fort Pierce, founded in 1837 during the Second Seminole War, retains a touch of old Florida at the same time that the boom transforms parts of it and Stuart, which calls itself the sailfish capital of the world, into a northward extension of the Gold Coast. Among the treasured artifacts of Fort Pierce history are gold and silver coins, some preserved in local museums, salvaged from Spanish treasure ships wrecked by storms just off the coast. The most exclusive community between Palm Beach and Vero Beach may be Hobe Sound, where the residents have wealth to rival that of Palm Beach, but are so devoted to privacy that

The fascinating series of islands called the Florida Keys stretch 150 miles through the ocean south of Miami in

a gentle curve that ends at Key West. Here, the soft glow of an afternoon sun trails away from tiny Sands Key.

the public rarely has an opportunity to ogle it.

Along the Gold Coast, it all appears golden, and it is folly to compare. Yet, even if that is so, the oldest and most honored gold resides in Palm Beach, across Lake Worth from the commercial city Henry Flagler created, West Palm Beach. Here there is an elegance which none other reaches. Rolls Royces and Mercedes roll up and down streets and homes where the lawns and hedges and trees appear to have been combed and coiffed and manicured. Even the waters along the beach look bluer. The post office sports impressive but not gaudy gold lettering. Mailboxes have no names and the great houses have a regal air. Rarely will a tourist see so many signs warning him not to do something. Just to glide through those tree-shaded streets, and gaze on that clipped perfection, can afford one a fresh empathy with the Crackers. This is where the Swells live.

The name Palm Beach sprang from an accident. A Spanish ship loaded with Havana coconuts wrecked offshore in 1878. About 14,000 coconuts washed ashore. Early settlers planted them, and eight years later the palm population prompted adoption of the name.

If Henry Flagler's railroad and hotels transformed Palm Beach, the architect Addison Mizner gave it an Old World shape and style. Like so many others, Mizner came to Florida for his health. From 1918 through the roaring days of the Boom, the wealthy called on Mizner to build their temples. He responded with a lavish, ornate adaptation of Spanish architecture that created a Florida fad. A favorite story about Mizner cites the time an aide questioned the great costs of what he proposed to do. Mizner replied that Palm Beach clients could not bear anything that was not expensive.

Palm Beach became a well-bred way of life that attracted the wealthy and the powerful. It began with yachts and chauffeured limousines, priceless jewels and parties in the royal fashion. From there it zoomed off into informal summitry among diplomats, business giants and statesmen. John F. Kennedy knew Palm Beach both as a boy and as a man, and vacationed here as President.

For the visitor, a ride up and down County Road, Ocean Boulevard, Royal Palm Way and Royal Poinciana Way, a visit to the spiffy shops along Worth Avenue, sightseeing among the exclusive hotels, and a tour of the fabulous Flagler Museum (the marble mansion the old tycoon built for his third wife) on Whitehall Way will provide the flavor.

From Palm Beach to Miami Beach, a distance of about 70 miles, high-rise condominiums and hotels rise back of the beaches like a ridge of man-made mountains. The concentration of people and development, even to those familiar with Florida, continues to be a fresh surprise. These are the

In Key West, life turns on tourists and the sea

At the southernmost point in the United States, surrounded by water, Key West depends for its livelihood upon the skill of its fishermen and the quaintness of an island village that is one of the oldest in all Florida. In the upper picture, tourists examine conch shells that divers sell on the streets. At left, two shrimpboats dock along a waterfront that includes restaurants waiting for the day's catch. At right, a fisherman dumps his load of freshly caught shrimp into a water trough that will keep them fresh until the cook is ready to pop them onto a fire. Turtle steak and Key lime Pie also are Key specialties.

The Seven-Mile-Bridge, at left, Florida's longest, begins at Marathon Key and arches dramatically over the ocean seven miles to Bahia Honda Key. The great leap takes it across Little Pigeon Key, site for marine research.

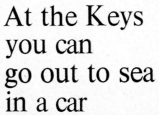

At the Keys you can go out to sea in a car

From millionaire yachtsmen to weekend fishermen, and tiny tots who only can wade all the way to professional scuba divers, the incomparable waters of the Florida Keys offer a special treat. A blend of sand, sky and ocean produce colors that vary with the tides and the course of the sun. Where the Gulf of Mexico and the Atlantic Ocean meet, fish are abundant.

In this house, lived Hemingway and his cats

Ernest Hemingway, the author, in 1931 bought this house in Key West which he owned until his death in 1961. Here he lived with his second wife Pauline and their two sons, and wrote such books as For Whom The Bell Tolls, A Farewell To Arms, The Snows of Kilimanjaro and The Macomber Affair.

The house at 907 Whitehead Street has been converted into a Hemingway Museum which tourists may visit and perhaps get a better understanding of how the writer lived. The spanish colonial house, at which Hemingway kept as many as fifty cats, was built of native rock and furnished with mementos from his

trips to Spain, Africa and Cuba. Exotic plants and trees shade the exterior, and Key West's first swimming pool was built in the backyard here, below his study. A catwalk connects the study with a porch in the rear of the house. Hemingway was the first major writer to settle in Key West, although many other writers later followed his choice.

The Hemingway family sold the home after his death, and it was opened to the public in 1964. Not only is the house a popular tourist stop because of Hemingway's great stature as a writer, but because it is considered a good example of local architecture.

An underseas park preserves the rare beauty of coral life

A diver hangs suspended in a flood of light, water and fish in John Pennekamp Coral Reef State Park, the first underseas park in the history of the United States. It was *created in 1960 to preserve the incredible beauty of underwater life in the Florida Keys. Its 77,000 square miles include the only living coral rock formations along the coast of North America. The park,*

named for conservationist
and editor John Pennekamp,
offers facilities for
expert and amateur
underwater enthusiasts.
There are glass-bottomed
boats for casual tourists
and even underwater
plastic guidebooks for
the more expert
who search for something
special. At lower
left, the nine foot bronze
statue, called Christ
Of The Deep,
is one point of interest.

backbone of the Gold Coast, and for many years made up the core of Florida's tourism attractions. Other Florida areas now might dispute that claim but for many the excitement and convenience of the Gold Coast with its fine restaurants and tourist accommodations, and varied nightlife, still symbolize the prestige vacation. Few places anywhere can match the range of attractions.

In all of Florida, each person will discover his own soul place. A whole chain of these developed and grew on the Gold Coast until they have formed a nearly solid metropolitan area. They are sprinkled along the way like gems. Below Palm Beach, there are Lake Worth, Boynton Beach, Delray Beach, Boca Raton, Deerfield Beach and Pompano Beach before you get to the striking resort city of Fort Lauderdale.

Boca Raton was built around a club designed by Addison Mizner for private membership but now operated as a hotel. The name comes from the Spanish for "rat's mouth," a phrase which the Spanish used to describe Boca Raton Sound. The community has survived as a refuge for the affluent, and is wellknown as a center for polo players. Less than 10 miles south of Boca Raton, tiny Hillsboro Beach at Lighthouse Point has an average family income that probably triples the state's average.

Fort Lauderdale earned a special niche in the Gold Coast. The fast-growing area has a reputation as the home of the Beautiful People, a modern name for the Swells, who enjoy both money and leisure. Highway A1A runs directly along the beaches, between the hotels and the Atlantic Ocean, providing free and full access for the public. College students by the thousands gather on the sands here during spring vacations, and in themselves become a spectacle which draws their elders to observe the antic rites.

Fort Lauderdale was another of those Florida cities whose name and beginnings came from the Second Seminole War. A few days after the Seminoles ambushed and massacred Maj. Francis L. Dade and his men near Bushnell (in December, 1835), five persons (including three children) were killed by Indians near here. Maj. William Lauderdale commanded a group of Tennessee militia sent to found a fort, which was named for him.

About 300 miles of canal criss-cross through modern Fort Lauderdale, called the Venice of America. Tourists may take cruise boats through the waterways for a better look at unusual homes. Remarkable yachting facilities, particularly those at oceanside Bahia Mar, make the city a yachting capital. Surveys suggest that Fort Lauderdale may have more yachts per capita than any other city in Florida. Nearby Port Everglades, one of the largest and busiest in Florida, is a principal stop for Caribbean cruise ships.

Pennekamp makes tour of 'his' state park

John Pennekamp, also known as the 'Father Of Everglades National Park', here visits the underwater park at Key Largo that bears his name. As a forceful editor on The Miami Herald, Pennekamp pioneered Florida's park system. Of him, former Gov. Leroy Collins once said,"To see his living monuments, you have only to look about you".
The park helps keep alive, and available to the public, a unique part of Florida's beauty.

Skippers who sail their yachts into Biscayne Bay can dock at marinas that put them only a short ride (or perhap

ly a short walk) from downtown Miami. In the shadow of that skyline are spread a park, library and bandshell.

In Florida, lifestyle emphasizes the outdoors

Man-made canals curve around tiny islands in which South Florida homes are set like so many jewels. An attentive sun permits Floridians the joy of open dwellings that combine shelter and a sense of outdoor living. Even on the bay, living rooms and patios extend to the edge of swimming pools. Just beyond will be the docks. The scene below shows a view of gardens from the upper floors of the Fontainebleau Hotel on Miami Beach.

Southwest of Fort Lauderdale, near Dania and Hollywood, is the smallest (480 acres) of the three Seminole reservations. Descendants of the Indians that fought for survival early in the 19th century now successfully pursue tourism and other commercial ventures in lands once considered remote and worthless.

The Gold Coast comes to an end in the sprawling complex of cities generally known as Miami (the most politically liberal city in Florida) but which in fact contains more than two dozen municipalities loosely joined in a metropolitan government. Miami, the most cosmopolitan city in the U.S. South and high among the most glamorous in the nation, has some of everything. To reach these distinctions, of course, you must include those other cities, beginning with Miami Beach, Coral Gables and Hialeah. They are part of the extraordinary mix that give it the appropriate nickname, The Magic City. However, the other cities insist upon remaining distinct and separate entities.

Miami Beach furnishes most of the glamor, the hotels and the nightlife. The great entertainers come here, both to appear in the nightclubs and to film movies or to stage television shows. Humorist Arthur Godfrey in earlier years and later comedian Jackie Gleason became adopted sons. The concentration of excellent hotels and restaurants, as well as the spacious facilities of the adjoining Miami Beach Convention Hall and Auditorium, make it a premier convention city. The hotels look more like palaces, and a drive down Collins Ave. at night unfolds a lighted fantasy of neon.

Long, low causeways connect Miami Beach to the mainland, with a series of small, fashionable residential islands resting in Biscayne Bay between the two cities. Bus and boat tours, plus blimp and helicopter rides, probably offer the stranger his best opportunity for seeing both Miami and Miami Beach. The most exclusive of the islands runs along Indian Creek, a waterway parallel to Collins Ave. which forms the western border of Miami Beach. Just as Miami benefits in reputation from satellite cities, so to some extent does Miami Beach. From south beach at Government Cut (the channel to the Port of Miami), Miami Beach runs about 90 blocks north. Then a series of smaller communities, beginning with Surfside, continues up the beach until they bump into the Fort Lauderdale area development coming south. The lower portion of Miami Beach, developed first, serves as a retirement haven for senior citizens. More fashionable hotels take over the upper beach, although an increasing number of them are converting to the condominium trade which buys rather than rents apartments. End to end, the shrubbed and flowered parks and streets of the beach cities share natural beauty with fascinations

For the older, the charms of Miami Beach may lie in the winter warmth and comfort and easy conversation with fellow travelers of similar vintage. The younger frequently prefer open stretches of beach, thatch-roofed huts and the light roll of surf. Here, daydreams and recreation alternate or blend nicely.

While golfers steer their carts up sleek fairways in Coral Gables, south of Miami, an athletic young man does a handstand on Miami Beach. Ladies, wielding parasols to avoid a sunburn, survey the scene. In South Florida, there's a place and a time for almost everybody under the sun. The trick is to choose what fits you best.

In the sun, a place for all, old or young

for the window-shopper. The eight-block long Lincoln Rd. mall, where trams help ferry the weary, and the Bal Harbour district shops may be the best known, but there are others along Collins Ave., Arthur Godfrey Rd., and in the individual communities and the hotels.

Once the visitor adjusts to the impact of the tropical climate and its variety of opportunities for recreation and leisure, the next most striking thing about the Miami area may be its international flavor. Political and other refugees from all over Latin America, but especially from Cuba, have settled here in what seems to them the city both closest and most conveniently within reach of home. Miami always had a touch of the Latin, because of its airport and seaport gateways to the lower half of the Western Hemisphere, but the flood of Cuban refugees since 1959 has transformed it. During a period of 15 years, more than a half million Cubans came to the United States, and most of these settled in or around Miami. They have made it bilingual, injected Latin soul and character into what had been a city of such mixed population and purpose that its character had been almost impossible to define. Cuban nightclubs, Cuban restaurants, Cuban grocery stores, Cuban politicians, Cuban radio stations and newspapers and an endless string of other Cuban businesses not only cluster in a "Little Havana" section of Miami, but spread throughout the area. Coral Gables, the plush residential city George Merrick founded southwest of Miami, has been a beneficiary too. The supply of bilingual Cubans has been a factor in helping make that city the "Corporate Capital of the Americas." Already the home of the University of Miami, and the "Miracle Mile" shopping district, Coral Gables thus has become international headquarters for firms doing business in the Caribbean and Latin America.

Downtown Miami fronts on Biscayne Bay. Its tallest buildings look across Biscayne Boulevard and Bayfront Park toward the Port of Miami on Dodge Island and beyond that toward Miami Beach. Key Biscayne, which has the look of a South Seas island, sits just offshore to the south with a causeway linking it to the city. The old Cape Florida lighthouse, first built in 1825, marks a 900-acre state park at the end of the key. Public beaches there and in Crandon Park make Key Biscayne a vacationer's delight. In recent years, the key also drew additional national attention as one of the "winter White Houses" during the administrations of former President Richard M. Nixon.

One of Miami's principal tourist attractions is a 16th century Venetian palace with 10 acres of formal gardens, that rises off Biscayne Bay like a European dream. It is called Vizcaya, after the Spanish province on the Bay of Biscay. James

Deering, a co-founder of the International Harvester Co., began its construction in 1912 from coral rock quarried nearby. Using stonecutters, artisans and gardeners from Italy, the palace was completed in five years. The Dade County (Miami) Park and Recreation Department now operates it as a museum.

The Monastery of St. Bernard in North Miami Beach originally was built at Segovia, Spain, in 1141, where it stayed until 1925. William Randolph Hearst bought it, had it dismantled stone by stone and shipped to the United States. After 26 years in stoarge, it was purchased from the Hearst estate, reassembled, and opened to the public.

Part of Miami now, but once an independent village, is Coconut Grove, a quaintly old Florida community with a mixed flavor of Bohemia and affluence. It has been called a tropical Greenwich Village.

Spectator sports are dominated by professional (the Miami Dolphins) and collegiate (the University of Miami) football teams. In a slightly different category are the pari-mutuel sports, where wagering on horses, dogs and jai alai is legal. These have proliferated over Florida, but particularly in the south. The practical city of Hialeah, incorporated in 1921, became the home of the Hialeah Race Course in 1931 when pari-mutuel betting was legalized. It was developed as a showplace as well as Florida's premier horse track, with grounds lined by royal palms, a broad selection of plants and flowers and an infield converted into a home for beautiful pink flamingoes. Even when the horses aren't running, it is a tourist attraction.

Where the Gold Coast ends, a whole new Florida begins. The city of Homestead, created by Flagler's railroad, is the gateway. Rich black soil along the edge of the Everglades makes Homestead, a prime area for citrus and avocado groves, and winter vegetables. The U.S. Air Force has a major base here. Below Homestead, the rocky Keys begin to spin out into the ocean in one of Florida's most spectacular sights.

The Keys draw mystery from legends of such pirates as Black Caesar and Blackbeard, who operated in the Florida straits. These combine with tales of the wreckers and salvagers of later years who grew wealthy from merchant ships that cracked up on the offshore reefs. Finally, there are the stories of men lured to the Keys by the strange geography, the balmy breezes and killer hurricanes, and by the close ties to the days when existence depended upon nature. All these fire the imagination, and as the Keys attracted artists and writers who live by their imagination, the mystique never seemed to weaken. Besides that, the Keys have exceptional fishing, and fishermen never have been known for understatement.

Sports aplenty, whether you play or just watch

Thoroughbred greyhounds kick up the dirt as they round the turn in races at Miami. Pari-mutuel sports, which means you can bet, include horse racing and the basque game of jai alai. In the picture at lower right the camera catches baseball action in a game at the University of Miami. University athletics, especially football, play a major role in spectator sports for South Florida fans.

The Gold Coast begins at Palm Beach and runs south until it stops at Miami Beach, the single most widely known place in Florida. Hotels, restaurants and nightclubs concentrated here probably make up one of America's most glamorous strips of oceanfront. At right, an aerial view shows how Indian Creek parallels the beach.

Along here, the famed Gold Coast sparkles

Although Miami Beach by reputation has become a sophisticated resort, all of it was built upon the sand, the sea and a gentle climate where a bikini feels fine in December and palm-lined beaches let a sailor pretend he's on the South Seas.

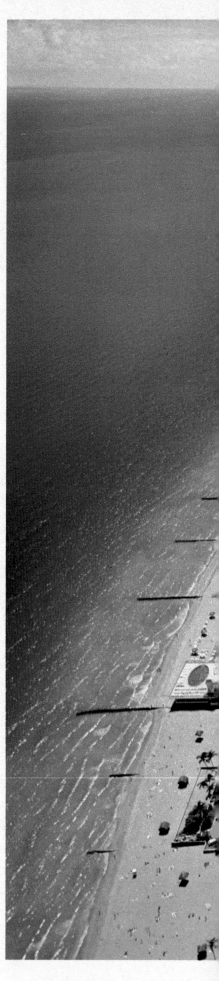

Not a crab claw, but a man playing jai alai

A jai alai player skids across the floor as he falls reaching for a shot. In jai alai, a spectator sport in Florida, the player wields a basket (called a cesta) tied to his arm, and catches in it a pelota (ball) which he bounces of a wall. There is some resemblance to handball, but aficionados or fans are quick to insist that jai alai (pronounced hi-li) is more difficult, more dangerous and far faster a game than handball. Jai alai frontons (as the courts are called) have begun to spread throughout the state.

Back in 1929, according to one story, a fellow named R. C. Perky planned to eradicate mosquitoes on the Keys. It would help business at his fishing resort. Perky built two 40-foot bat towers, one of which still stands, and staffed them with imported Cuban bats. His plan supposedly was for the bats to range out and eat the mosquitoes, and then return to the bat towers until they got hungry again. But when he opened the louvered doors for the first hunt, the bats simply flew away. The mosquitoes stayed.

The story of the modern Keys principally revolves around the Flagler railroad, later to become the Overseas Highway, but the Keys and Key West existed long before that. The first permanent settlers came to Key West in 1822, and at one time it was both the largest and wealthiest city in Florida. Despite the railroad, modern systems of transportation diminished the importance of Key West's southernmost location in the United States.

From Key Largo at the top of the Keys, down the full 108 miles to Key West (seven miles of it on just one bridge, Florida's longest), past the little roadside stands and honkytonks and restaurants and fishing camps, the Keys are an incredible mix of rock, sand and sea. Only what nature put here seems to rest easy – the bright glare off the sea, the thick smell of the salt air, the flat islands and the dazzling blue-green waters.

In addition to the other assets of the other Keys, Key Largo boasts the unique John Pennekamp Coral Reef State Park, an underseas park that includes nearly 100 miles of the only living coral reef formations on the U.S. coasts. It preserves, and opens to the public, the sparkling beauty of underwater marine and plant life in the Keys. John Pennekamp, for years a forceful editor for The Miami Herald, led the crusade to create the park. He also earned the reputation as the Father of the Everglades National Park, for his work in making that longtime dream of conservationists come true. The two parks now are regarded among the United States' greatest natural treasures.

In the Keys the oldtime residents, many of whom descended from Bahamians, are called Conchs. The conch is a large shellfish which divers find on the reefs. The fish itself is edible in salads, chowder, or fried into conch fritters, and the shells are sold as souvenirs. But a human Conch is simply an oldtimer, and the nickname is complimentary.

Key West is a city of the old and the new. Ernest Hemingway once lived here (his home is now a tourist attraction) and found inspiration for his books. Playwright Tennessee Williams made it home. Former President Harry Truman established his "winter White House" here at the U.S. Naval Base. The Navy has gone now, but the Air Force remains. Along the eastern end of the island,

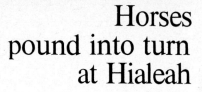

Horses pound into turn at Hialeah

When horse race season begins at south Florida's tracks, millions of tourists and bettors flock to the charts and racing forms to determine where to place their faith and dollars. Here *at right, the camera freezes a charge of thoroughbreds as they round a turn at Hialeah Race Course. Jockeys lean forward to urge greater speed, while listening for the sound of challenging hoofs*

coming up from behind. During a strain of a race, the rippling muscles of the horses pop out like ridges, the nostrils flare and the mouth foams as each animal tries to excel in the thing for which he was bred: speed. At left, before the race, fans study the horses as they are led from the stables to the track, and check past records hoping to find a clue to today's winners.

At finish, hooves fly as railbirds wave, shout

A breeze whips through the infield palms, making the flag flutter in the background as the toteboard gleams with the final odds. Fans along the rail lean over like a row of roosting birds to shout encouragement to their favorites as the horses come thundering home at Hialeah's finish line. Along that rail, there is ecstasy and anguish at the end of each race.

on broad Roosevelt Blvd., the new dominates. There is the flash of neon and the rise of concrete. Old Key West at the other end, the part best loved by the Conchs, has narrow streets that run past ancient frame houses with gingerbread trimming. The little frame homes with tiny fenced yards, remnants of the past, are called Conch houses. Old Key West's buildings have been restored to please the tourists and the Conchs too.

From Key West, there is only one way to go in Florida – north. West of Miami and Homestead are the great Everglades. Marjorie Stoneman Douglas called them The River of Grass in a book that bore that title. They are unique. There is nothing in the world to compare with them. From Lake Okeechobee, the land tilts slightly south, pushing the inches-deep waters slowly down a 50-mile wide path through vast fields of tall sawgrass (as high as 12 feet) into conservation areas that supply south Florida and sustain an irreplaceable heritage of wildlife and vegetation. A network of drainage canals and dikes helps both to store the water, and to reclaim swamplands for agriculture. It is a delicate balance, not always precisely maintained. During periods of drought, parts of the Everglades wither and dry while the water is being saved for human purposes. Great fires sometimes roar through the hammocks and trees, destroying shelter and food for the wildlife.

The Everglades National Park covers 1.4 million acres where rare creatures and plants thrive. Alligators and crocodiles, bald eagles and roseate spoonbills, egrets and wood storks, snook and tarpon and shrimp, royal palm and mahogany and cypress trees flourish. You can best sample the wonders of the Everglades by beginning at the Flamingo Visitor Center, on Florida 27 southwest of Homestead. Rangers offer advice on canoe trails, boating facilities, campgrounds, fishing and nature trails. Park service ranger stations in the Keys can tell you of the boating possibilities around Cape Sable, at the southwest tip of Florida, and up the coast among the Ten Thousand Islands. The Wilderness Waterway, a 99-mile boating trail, runs northwest from Flamingo to Everglades City, the western gateway to the park. On the north side of the park, on U.S. 41 at Shark Valley, a public transportation system takes visitors on a loop deep into the freshwater sloughs and sawgrass for a view of the wildlife.

Lake Okeechobee, so surrounded by dikes that you cannot see it from the highways that link the perimeter cities of Clewiston, Pahokee, Belle Glade and Okeechobee, feeds the Everglades from 730 square miles of shallow waters. The black mucklands surrounding the lake gradually "burn away" or evaporate when the water is drained from them. The uniquely rich soil supports winter vegetable farms and commercial sugar operations. A little farther off the lake, cattle take advantage

A flock of rare and beautiful flamingos, not often seen elsewhere in Florida, make their home at Hialeah Race Course. The long-legged birds lend exceptional color to the track infield and are one reason why Hialeah and its grounds are a worthwhile tourist stop even in the offseason when the horses are not running. At right, the picture shows the graceful birds in flight against a dark background of palms and other trees. All south Florida's horse tracks, including Calder near Hollywood and Gulfstream in Hallandale, have developed their individual attractions but Hialeah, oldest of the three, remains the classic example.

Always in the pink at Hialeah

of extensive, flat grasslands as pastures. The Okeechobee Waterway beginning at Stuart on the east coast runs through the lake and across to the Caloosahatchee River and Fort Myers, linking the Gulf and the Atlantic.

The Seminole Indians' two other reservations take up areas of the Everglades, where their ancestors once found refuge, and Lake Okeechobee flat lands. The Big Cypress reservation (42,728 acres) sits almost in the center of the Everglades but north of that portion that is the park. The Brighton reservation (35,805 acres), known for its investment in the cattle industry, is located just off the northwestern shore of the lake.

Fifty years after the Second Seminole War, old Fort Harvie at the mouth of the Caloosahatchee River had been replaced by the larger Fort Myers, named for Col. Abraham C. Myers. About that time, in 1885, Thomas A. Edison discovered the charms of the place. That was six years after he invented the electric lamp.

Edison came to Fort Myers looking for a bamboo filament for his lamp that would burn longer than a few hours. Enchanted with Fort Myers, he established a winter home here along the river, built a laboratory and then boasted: "There is only one Fort Myers, and 90 million people are going to find out about it." Edison spent 46 winters here, laboring over the 1,097 patented inventions that he produced. Because of him, such business giants as Henry Ford and Harvey Firestone became acquainted with Fort Myers. Ford bought the house next door and Firestone sponsored Edison's research into a rubber substitute (finally developed from goldenrod).

Today the old Edison home, deeded to the city by his widow, probably ranks as the city's greatest man-made tourist attraction. Some of his old bamboo filament light bulbs still burn in the house. During the early days, Edison's visitors could reach his home only by boat, and for sometime after 1905 only by railroad. Not until 1928 was an overland route established across the Everglades to link Miami directly with Fort Myers and the rest of the west coast of Florida.

A 10-car expedition guided by Indians tried the trip first in 1923. Three weeks later, seven cars showed up in Miami. Five years later the Tamiami (Tampa to Miami) Trail was opened up. As U.S. 41, it still is one of the two highways that cut through the great sawgrass swamps. The other, called Alligator Alley, runs from Fort Lauderdale directly through the Biy Cypress Seminole reservation to Naples on the gulf.

Along the Tamiami Trail out of Miami, another group of Seminoles pursues the tourist business with perhaps a more hardsell approach than their reservation cousins. Dressed in the traditional brightly colored, loose clothing, their roadside stands advertise airboat rides into the Ever-

Vizcaya now operates as a museum, owned by Dade County. The 70-room palace and its furnishings, plus the 52-acre tract of land and gardens, are open every day except Christmas. The name comes from the Spanish Basque province Vizcaya, which was located appropriately on the Bay of Biscay. The estate's gardens reach to a private harbor which fronts on Miami's Biscayne Bay.

When wealthy James Deering decided in 1914 that he should retire, he chose Coconut Grove on the outskirts of Miami. He brought in more than 1,000 craftsmen, including Italian stonecutters, and had this magnificent old Italian-style mansion built. It resembles Italy's 16th century fortress-palaces. After five years of construction Deering entered his new home on Christmas day, 1916. The stone was quarried and cut from Florida's native coral, and carved to Deering's specifications. Its formal gardens and unique buildings make Vizcaya one of the great houses in America.

Amid Miami's modern scene, an old palace

Key Biscayne showtime: where fish perform

With an early morning start, deep-sea fishing boats churn far off the Florida coast hunting for the big ones. By the time the sun goes down, many have found them.

Across Florida there are large and remarkable aquariums where rare fish not only live but perform with the zest and skill of Broadway stars. Among these are Marine Studios, Sea World and on Key Biscayne, the Seaquarium. Each displays marine life. Probably the most popular are the killer whales, shown leaping through a water ballet at right. In the picture above, a girl crouches and puts her head into a whale's mouth.

A fisherman carefully lifts an angry shark, hook still trailing from its mouth, into the boat. A day's foray into deep waters off the coast of Florida, including the Gulf Stream, can produce a variety of catch that might range from bait fish to a man-sized battler. Such a monster sometimes can make the struggle to land him seem a good day's work.

83

To put south Florida's island-flanked coast in perspective, busloads of children take to the air in the Goodyear blimp. From that height they can see the causeways to Miami Beach, the cruise ships in port and Key Biscayne a short hop to the south. Here, the Keys begin to follow the point of Florida, until land stops and they skip out into the ocean like stepping stones for a giant.

Strolling along the bay, or picnicking near the old lighthouse in Key Biscayne's Cape Florida park, you may find a shell in which you can always hear the ocean's roar. Shells are souvenirs with sound systems.

Find the sea in a blimp, or a shell

glades; visits to Indian villages with the frond-roofed chickees; gift shops filled with trinkets and handcrafts; and sometimes wildlife exhibits or alligator wrestling matches.

No one gets lost on the Trail anymore, as did the 1923 pioneers, but there are sufficient diversions on the route to slow you down. You pass the town of Ochopee, which proclaims it has the United States' smallest post office (eight feet, four inches by seven feet, three inches) and move into the county named for Barron Gift Collier, another of Florida's pioneer promoters. Collier made a fortune in streetcar advertising, and poured it into southwest Florida real estate. His headquarters was Everglades City, now the western gateway to the Everglades National Park and a fishing village. Among his historic accomplishments, before he died broke in 1939, Collier helped a reluctant state government finance the construction of the Tamiami Trail.

Offshore from Everglades City, at the northern tier of the Ten Thousand Islands, is Chokoloskee Island. Once inhabited by the Calusa Indians, who left large shell mounds, Chokoloskee now caters to commercial fishermen. A causeway built in 1955 links it to the mainland.

A few miles north, Marco Island contrasts sharply with Chokoloskee, though it too was favored by the Calusas. Marco, with two causeways to the mainland, has been developed into a resort and convention city. It has modern homes, fine tourist accommodations and clusters of high-rise condominiums.

When the Tamiami Trail opened the way for Fort Myers, it changed the way of life in Naples, too. Now both the Trail and Alligator Alley (to Fort Lauderdale) link it with the south and east. Naples had been settled as a winter resort late in the 19th century by a group of Kentuckians who named it for the city in Italy. After the passing of the Depression in the 1930's, the beaches and climate and quieter atmosphere of the lower southwest coast drew migrants of means looking for an orderly way of life in the sun. Naples, a planned city, answered that desire. Its wide streets, trim and attractive shopping areas, gave it a touch of the sedate character the Swells found appealing. The rush of development has tended to democratize but not spoil that tendency.

Between Naples and Fort Myers, in addition to the appeal of the gulf coast beaches, there are two other unique spots. In Estero, a religious group called Koreshan Unity established headquarters a few years after Naples was established. They practiced the communal life and believed that people existed on the inside of the earth, rather than on its surface, and that the sun hung somewhere in the open middle. Modern space exploration altered but did not eliminate these theories.

Layer after layer of Miami expressways lace together a metropolitan area that blankets two dozen smaller cities and surrounding suburbs with a downtown core to which most workers must commute daily.

Many Cuban refugees settled in southwest Miami, and transformed one area along the Tamiami Trail into "Little Havana". The Cuban influence extends almost everywhere, however, and broad use of Spanish has made this an officially recognized bilingual city. The Cuban flavor has injected a touch of Latin soul into Miami life and brought new business vigor.

Miami: tropical, modern and Latin

Elderly Cubans sit on the sidewalks and play checkers, just as they once did on the island they still refer to as home. The Cuban impact on Miami has introduced some of the very human Latin qualities that stress in emotional ways an emphasis on family, home, and old friends as well as tolerance for man's problems and imperfections. The Cuban presence has heightened the attraction of Miami as a tourist city. Food and service at Cuban restaurants often exemplify an old world style rarely found. The Cubans, in effect, have created a city of their own within Miami.

The Corkscrew Swamp Sanctuary has a rare and different appeal. It is located west of Bonita Springs, on Florida 846, and offers opportunity to walk through a virgin cypress forest perhaps seven centuries old. A board walkway provides access to the Lettuce Lakes, and to the swamp where the Seminoles made their last stand. Wildlife lives here unmolested, including nesting egrets, alligators, otters and raccoons.

West of Fort Myers are two of Florida's most beautiful islands, Sanibel and Captiva. Until 1964, they offered seclusion, uncluttered beaches, incomparable varieties of shells washed up by the usually gentle waves of the gulf and a way of life divorced from the crowds. A toll causeway linked the islands to the mainland that year, increasing the rate of development and modifying the seclusion, but they remain a favorite hideaway for swimmers, fishermen, artists, writers and those seeking only a place both warm and quiet. The 5,000 acre wildlife sanctuary, a favorite gathering place for birdwatchers, assures a degree of that peace will be permanent.

North of Fort Myers, at Charlotte Harbor where the Peace River flows into the gulf, is the area where Ponce de Leon came on his second trip in 1513 and collected a fatal Indian arrow. On one side of the harbor is Punta Gorda and on the other side Port Charlotte. Punta Gorda historically has been a shipping point for fish and vegetables. A developer created Port Charlotte from a cattle range in the mid-1960's and it became popular among retirees.

Across Charlotte Harbor on Gasparilla Island (named for Jose Gaspar, a pirate supposed to have operated along the gulf coast in the 19th century), the town of Boca Grande (Spanish for "big mouth") draws sports fishermen looking for tarpon, snook, sea trout and other game fish that thrive in the harbor and nearby waters.

If Florida were a cake, The Magical South would be its sweet icing. It lives below the frostline, and frolics year-round if it chooses. Most of the economy is based upon tourism, and so there is at least a surface concentration on pleasure and recreation. Beneath all that froth, though, year-round residents work and worry and pay taxes just like everybody else. You are more likely to see them in the parks and campgrounds, or boating and fishing in the ocean and along the canals, than in the nightclubs or the specialized tourist attractions. Most of them once were tourists here, too, and they have seen the sights. Some say that you can spot the tourist by his suntan, but that is not true. You are more likely to spot him by his sunburn. The natives learned long ago to cultivate the sun gradually rather than try to capture it in one weekend and take it back home.

In Florida south, the sun is a year-round resident, too, and you learn to live with it.

In Palm Beach all that glitters is golden

If you want to see how the very wealthy live and play, you can peek through the fences and hedges, drive down the palm-lined streets, or ogle into the shops and the many show windows of elegant Palm Beach. You can't see it all, but you will get the idea. At right, a view of yachts anchored in Lake Worth, looking toward Palm Beach.

A fallen tree arches high out of waters near the Everglades not far from Flamingo to frame a mangrove tree on the shoreline

In the tangled roots and branches of these mangroves, a unique system of wildlife finds natural protection, food and shelter.

The Everglades: dark, mysterious and beautiful

As far as you can see, the untracked Everglades spread across millions of acres of south Florida. Its shallow waters seep slowly through the grasses and around the hammocks until they reach the Gulf of Mexico. For years, they were regarded as impenetrable, but now man encroaches as much as laws permit.

A canoe is the proper way to explore the Everglades, for you can move silently, disturbing little, and hear all the sounds of the great swamp. The bellow of a bull alligator, or the sweet call of a multi-hued bird, merge into a thousand other noises that seem to harmonize with rather than to shatter the sense of tranquility. A fish swirls in the reeds, a bird splashes in the shallows, a bobwhite whistles to its mate. These are not the intruders; you are.

During drought, 'glades dry, crack, burn

*The magic, and
the life, of the Everglades
depend upon the flow
of water. When a drought
stems or stops that flow,
the mud flats grow dry and
split into hard
patches to form patterns
that look like lines
on a map. The wildlife
retreats or dies.
A strike of lightning or a
carelessly dropped
cigaret can start a blaze
that will incinerate
hundreds of acres. During
the rainy season,
more than three-fourths
of the Everglades
is made up of water.*

A cloud of birds whips off the Everglades flats, like a swiftly rising storm in the summer, their urgently beating wings making a

ataplan of sound. They flutter across a line of dark trees in the background, for one brief instant stitching it with flashes of white

Shafts of sunlight break through to make soft patterns in a typical scene where trailing whiskers of Spanish moss hang from

ypress trees whose ridged trunks grow in Everglades muck beside swamp waters covered with blossoming hyacinths.

*A dignified pelican
finds himself an A-frame
perch where he may
contemplate the scene as
befits a gentleman
who wishes to satisfy curios-
ity without seeming
to be commonly nosy. That
'46' is not his
house address, but a number
for this channel
marker, which boaters
find significant
if they wish to come out
of the Everglades
as easily as they came in.*

All life in the Everglades does not swim or fly, though it often seems so. The picture at left shows a flowering air plant that has found a way to survive without either getting its feet wet or having to grow wings. In the upper picture, more typical residents take the Florida sun in leisurely fashion. While the dark waters around them reflect a true jungle rising around their little pond, the turtles bask and ponder what unwary fish will provide the entree for the evening's dinner. The irreplaceable beauty of the Everglades, say ecologists, lies in the unique chain of life which sustains and feeds upon itself, from one-celled animals up through the fish to the alligator, bobcat and black bear. They need each other.

For each, a way, and a place in nature

Water ripples away from the flat nose of an alligator as he glides through the Everglades' black waters toward possible prey. Ey

ed and glowering primitively, ridged back fully surfaced, the 'gator quietly gives the impression of untamed jungle ferocity.

In Everglades, the law makes wildlife king

A pelican spreads its wings like a feathery airliner, and splashes to an Everglades roost. Here in this watery wilderness, only nature limits the wildlife. Laws protect the birds and animals as well as their environment. Man's thunderous development remains a rumble in the far distance, but the sound grows.

Without wings or fins, your best passage into the 'glades will be by airboat, but there are few trails to follow here. When a boat passes, the sawgrass closes back in and the track disappears. Paths remain only as long as boats run regularly. Guides can follow rivers, hammocks.

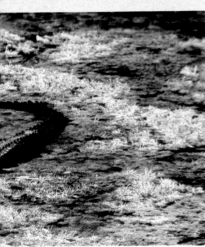

A propellor pushes the airboat across sawgrass or mud flats with ease, as though it were an airplane that does not fly. With an airboat, nearly all the millions of acres are easily accessible to park rangers. Visitors will enjoy the canoe trails through the deeper water. Canoes may offer better approach to the wildlife.

Fort Lauderdale: mecca for college students on holiday

During school vacations the beautiful public beaches of Fort Lauderdale attract thousands of students pursuing a suntan, companionship and escape to leisure. At Fort Lauderdale, Highway A1A runs directly along the ocean, offering unusual public access to one of the prettiest stretches of beach on the Gold Coast. When the students begin to cavort in the spring, the result is a show that even the older enjoy. It is a circus without animals, just people.

Yachting is a way of life in Fort Lauderdale, where boats are as common as cars. Here, a view from the top of the mast as one skipper unfurls the U.S. flag and makes ready to cruise out for deep-sea fishing along the Gulf Stream.

Where you can park beneath the palms

A sailboat rides the waves offshore, as cars search for parking places beneath the palms along Fort Lauderdale beach. Below, the sun toasts a young lady well-done. At right, the sands become a bed, a pillow or a round-table for discussing the merits of bikini-clad passersby. Some prefer to promenade rather than to swim, surf or loll about on the sand talking and ogling.

Canals lace Lauderdale like streets

An aerial view of Fort Lauderdale makes it easy to understand why the city is called the Venice of America. A latticework of canals brings the waterfront to many doorsteps, and boaters (such as those at left) have almost endless waterways to explore. Because luxury and leisure combine so impressively here, attracting those who can afford to enjoy both, Fort Lauderdale also carries the enviable status of being known as the home of The Beautiful People.

Taking advantage of smooth seas and a cloudless sky, sailboats from the Fort Lauderdale area cluster for an ocean rende

zvous. In the foreground, an interloping powerboat speeds by. For all type boats and boaters, Florida offers year-round sport.

Sculptors of sand decorate the beach

With an entire beach to shape and mold, young and old artists find inspiration at every turn on Fort Lauderdale beach. First, the sand is patted into form, and then the colors are added. Faces and situations reflect the limitless imaginations of those lighthearted and generous enough to create touches of beauty to be shared with passing strangers. Above, a red-jumpered parachutist floats serenely through a sky getting a fresh coat of blue. Below him there's an angry chick and a moonfaced cartoon character. At left, one artist finds it

necessary to label her
work. At day's
end, an exhibition of sand
sculpture rises
from the beach. This kind
of play requires a
special temperament, or
lack of it, for the
artist's creations are
passing fancies.
One scuff of a foot, or
the inevitable rise
of the tide, can ruin
instantly a masterpiece
that took hours
not just of thought but
labor under the
sun. Only a philosopher
could graciously
accept such a charitable
commission that
meant a too quick end
to his mind's child.
Yet, sand castles still rise.

Hollywood's port docks both big and small

Port Everglades, located just south of Fort Lauderdale in the city of Hollywood, is one of Florida's major ports. Caribbean passenger cruise ships, tankers and even the U.S. Coast Guard use the facilities. At left a local cruise ship, the Jungle Queen, steams under one of the area's several drawbridges. This water-oriented area found it necessary to build Florida's only vehicular tunnel so that the boats and drawbridges would not keep traffic seriously interrupted on the main highway through the city. Along the oceanfront, high-rise condominiums and hotels dominate the picturesque scene.

At Fort Lauderdale in the
spring, they hold
five days of balloon fashion
shows and racing to
benefit the Boys' Clubs of
America. The finale
features a classic journey to
the Bahama Islands
by balloon, with
a yacht convoy as escort.
The balloons are
launched at Holiday Park.

Racing balloons have
become part of the varied
Florida scene. If
horses and dogs and boats
and men can race,
why not balloons? At left,
as one balloon rises,
another inflates to join the
show. Above, one
gondola awaits a lift as con-
testants get ready and
spectators stand by for the
action. Just as sail
boats skimming across the
ocean set an unfor-
gettable Florida picture, so
now do balloons
float up into the clouds
and add a
new dimension both to sport
and the horizon.

They race
to Bahamas
in balloons

Balloons swell up like striped, airbone whales and take to the skies carrying men in swinging gondolas. For spo.

...d for charity, Fort Lauderdale holds an annual festival of balloon races, fashion shows and other social events.

Just off the gulf coast, between Naples and Fort Myers, the islands of Sanibel and Captiva are washed by tides that bring millions of shells to the shores. The experts say there are no better shelling beaches anywhere in the Western Hemisphere. Even those who come here to enjoy the natural beauty of the islands, soon find themselves walking the sands and stoping and squinting hoping to find a junonia or golden olive. It is a pastime that fascinates nearly all, both for the pleasure of the hunt and the exquisite beauty of the shells, too. Wildlife artists discover good subjects here.

At Sanibel Island, look for shells

One bird matches his beak against the horn of the rhino while the other bravely turns his back. The issue was resolved without the shedding of any feathers. At right, an ostrich and two parrots stand ready to testify in case there's a collision. In Florida the rhino is one more foreigner who found an interesting new life under the sun. These pictures taken at Lion Country Safari.

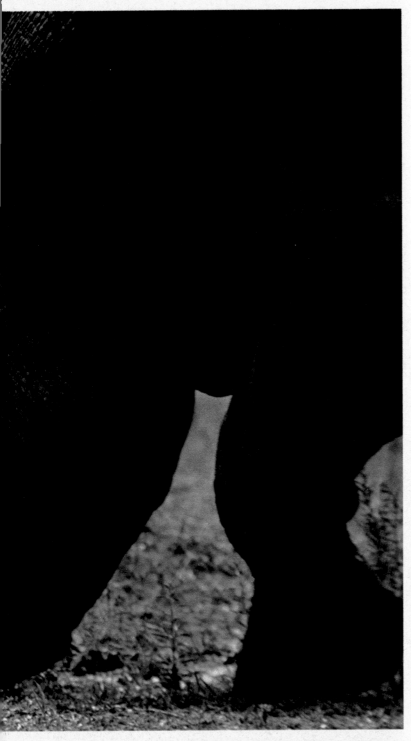

Even the cars have zebra stripes when the family takes a ride through a simulated African back country. In the picture below, one family on tour includes this commercial wildlife attraction on its long list of places to see in Florida. For variety and contrast, the state is hard to beat. Its other foreign flavors include Cuban, Greek, Czech, Bahamian and Spanish.

The big and little of it: a point for the rhino

Palms and pines make just as shady resting places as the trees back home in Africa, these lions discover. Here they may have more traffic but chances are life comes easier in their private compound.

Water cannons fire volleys at vegetables

As far as you can see, long, flat fields of south Florida's rich, black earth bring up vegetables in neat rows that look like pin-stripes. To nourish them, water cannons spray rainbow-like arches that moisten the tender leaves. During winter, fields around Homestead and Lake Okeechobee help keep U.S. dinner tables filled with beans, cucumbers, tomatoes and corn. Migrant workers harvest the crops.

127

Harvest time in sugar- cane fields

Cutting the tall stalks of sugarcane, and sending them to the mills for grinding, is difficult, back-breaking work. There are not many light moments in the fields, but the two lads at right discover diversion in catching a rabbit flushed from his cover by the cutters. Most of Florida's sugarcane is grown in the black earth that lies around giant Lake Okeechobee. Nearby sugar mills squeeze out the cane juices, process them into refined sugar.

Wielding a machete, the sugarcane worker at right slashes the stalks just above the ground and tosses them aside to be picked up and hauled to the mill. Because the machete blades must be sharp, workers easily can injure themselves if not careful. This fellow wears guards across his shins and feet to avoid accidents. Under a hot Florida sun, stooping to cut properly, the canecutters' work not only requires skill but unusual stamina. A cutting machine has been invented but not perfected.

Swamps don't stop these cars

Each year, at the Naples Swamp Buggy festivals, these versatile vehicles show just what they can do, and it is quite a lot. The balloon-wheeled, custom-made buggies are designed to cross almost any Everglades terrain.

As a crowd of several thousand watch, swamp buggies plow right through water and mud deep enough to submerge the entire vehicle. The pictures at left show how drivers may steer their incredible machines into such depths that only their heads and shoulders remain above the surface. At right, a buggy bursts out of the swamp, revealing the huge wheels that give it unusual traction and drive. The Naples festivals, held each summer and winter, have become popular events not only for tourists but for those interested in what's required if you wish to take a drive in the Everglades.

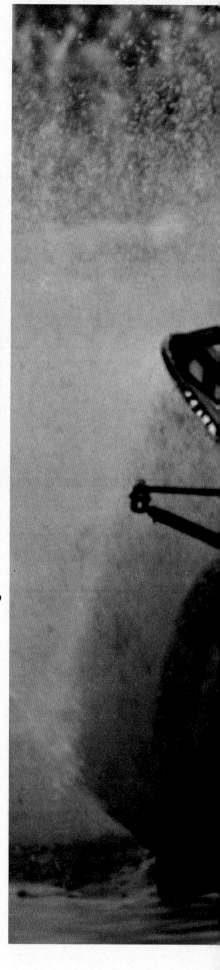

130

The Seminoles keep alive tribal tradition

On their three official reservations in Florida, the Seminole Indians try to retain examples of their traditional customs and living styles. These not only make a contribution to Florida tourism, but are valuable to historians and to the Indians themselves in preserving an important heritage. On their substantial land holdings, the Seminoles also raise cattle and are involved in other businesses. Pictures

here show a Seminole girl
cradling a baby in
a hammock, and a man
at work wood-carving.
Examples of Indian
handcrafts are sold both
at souvenir shops
on or near the reservations
and by another group
of Seminoles who live
along the Tamiami Trail
outside of Miami. At
right, the larger picture
illustrates what a
Seminole village once might
have looked like.
The thatch-roofed huts
are called 'chickees.'

Many families prefer to see Florida in their trailers or by pitching tents in the state's many parks and campgrounds. From

he Keys to Pensacola to Fernandina Beach, facilities abound for those who briefly want to sample the outdoor life

135

Florida Crackers,
and many others as well,
will tell you that
nothing beats a fresh fish
supper caught along
the bank of a canal or out
of giant Lake
Okeechobee. Whether you
fish from a folding
chair, or a plush houseboat,
it tastes the same.

A canepole can fetch a sizzling supper

Not everyone likes them,
but the Crackers say
that when you can fry your
own catfish in an iron
skillet over an open fire,
there's no better
tasting fish anywhere
under the sun.
The picture above shows
how it should be done.

The Bulging Middle

The full life gives Florida a nice spread across the middle. Interstate Highway 4 girds it like a fourlaned belt, from Daytona Beach on the east coast through Orlando and Lakeland and into Tampa and St. Petersburg. Explosive growth put a bulge around that belt. This is Central Florida, and we will define its northern boundary as slicing the state just above Daytona Beach on the Atlantic, Leesburg in the center and Crystal River on the gulf.

Here the lifestyle accommodates a touch of chill in the winter, fine bass-fishing lakes become numerous, oranges grow, phosphate is mined and big cattle ranches operate. Automobiles race at Daytona Beach, rockets fire off toward the moon at Cape Canaveral, Mickey Mouse makes his home at Walt Disney World, and the cities around Tampa Bay combine industry and a busy port with the task of keeping the tourists and retirees happy. If life seems less magical than in the south, it seems more real.

Orlando, where the north-south Florida Turnpike crosses I-4 running east-west, is the hub. Settled by cattlemen after the Second Seminole War, it developed into Florida's largest inland city, and one of its most attractive. Its city limits encircle dozens of lakes and parks. Orlando's central location always assured it a major role in the state, but the development of the space exploration program at Cape Canaveral in the 1950's and the opening of the 43-square mile Walt Disney World entertainment-recreational complex positively sent it soaring. Disney World's presence (20 miles southwest) brought other major attractions flocking into the area to take advantage of the traffic. The multiplying effect virtually rewrote the standing maxims on Florida tourism.

Disney World deals in fantasies, from the comfortable past to the exciting future. The present, and all its anxieties, get little emphasis. It is a happy place and, for the old as well as the young, creates a sense of well-being. You get the feeling that maybe the world is not going crazy, after all.

In almost every direction from Orlando, there is a special Florida treat. The possibilities for exploring and discovery are excellent for the tourist. There is neighboring Winter Park, site of Rollins College and some of the area's most impressive homes. Going north, you see Sanford, built along the shores of Lake Monroe and named for Gen. Henry S. Sanford (the man who helped persuade Hamilton Disston to save Florida from bankruptcy); and the tree-shaded university town of Deland, founded by Henry A. Deland in 1876. Deland in its early years offered citizens a tax rebate if they would plant trees. John B. Stetson, the hat maker, founded and endowed a university here that bears his name.

Daytona Beach built its own version of the Gold Coast with towering high-rise apartments and motels along a 23-mile stretch of broad (500 feet), flat, hard beaches. They call it The World's Most Famous Beach, and a fascinating variety of the unclothed young eat hot dogs on the sand, oil their sunburned bodies and walk the old Broadwalk like unappeased panthers. Overhead, small planes tug along red advertising streamers. The ferris wheel turns, the calliope plays and the fishing pier offers "hot bands and cold beer." On the often-crowded beaches, lifeguards rule with shrill whistles. Joggers splash through the wavelets making symbolically impermanent tracks. Dogs lead their owners about on leashes, dodging the sailing frisbees and slow-moving cars.

At the turn of the century, about 1902, some guests at the Ormond Beach Hotel (one of Henry Flagler's projects) started to race cars on the beaches. Within a year, a racing association was formed and speed buffs around the world began coming to Daytona Beach to test their specially

Modern Tampa towers in the background above Henry Plant's old Tampa Bay Hotel, which now houses the Unive

ity of Tampa. The minarets and the grand style of Plant's day still draw tourists to this striking historical landmark

built machines. In 1936, a year after England's Sir Malcolm Campbell set a record of 276 miles per hour in his famed Bluebird, a young racer named Bill France brought organization and promotion to the idea. He turned himself into a millionaire and gave Daytona Beach an extra drawing card. France got the racing off the beach in 1959 when he opened the Daytona Beach International Speedway just west of the city. Among a schedule of other events at different times of the year, the annual Speed Week in February fills the city at a time that used to be offseason. New Smyrna Beach, the neighbor to the south where Dr. Andrew Turnbull tried to establish the Mediterranean colony, caters to family groups and calls itself the World's Safest Beach.

Still farther down I-95 just 35 miles east of Orlando, the John F. Kennedy Space Center and Patrick Air Force Base near Cocoa and Cape Canaveral at times have focussed world attention on Florida. In 1961, major things started happening here. Man began firing himself into space inside bullets, and President Kennedy promised the moon. Nothing else in recent American history has been so visionary, or more inspiring. Now those pioneering years stay alive in museums at the space center.

Mission control for those early space shots, its blinking lights moving across world maps, still looks Buck Rogers enough to excite tourists. The first missile fired here, in 1950, an old German V-2 liberated from Hitler, stands in a field where rockets sprout like corn stalks. Each phase of the space program is represented. The giant vehicular assembly building, bigger than the United Nations and the Empire State buildings, dwarfs everything in sight. Nearby, the space vehicle transporter, called the largest vehicle in the world, keeps the pace. Within two hours in a tour bus, the visitor can see the monuments of that incredible space effort — which was crammed into such a few short years — spread across thousands of acres within sound of the Atlantic surf.

The contrast is exaggeratedly symbolic of all Florida. From frontier to museum did not take long, and the links between them show clearly and astoundingly. An old brick lighthouse first built in 1847 still stands. Orange groves, planted here long before the rockets came, still bear fruit. Rattlesnakes and birds and alligators thrive in the wildlife refuge on the space center. Like old Florida, which must adjust to the thunderous growth springing up on all sides, they survive in spite of change that surpasses anything that nature had expected of them.

The coastal cities of Titusville, Cocoa and Melbourne, all built along the Indian River, insist their oranges are Florida's sweetest and juiciest. Fruit here is labeled Indian River, and a promotional campaign has been built around the name.

Tampa moves ahead, but does not forget

Within sight of each other, the Plant Museum and a memorial to John F. Kennedy help Tampa to remember. At right, the camera looks to the future with this view of Tampa International Airport, one of the most modern in Florida. The city's seaport is a major shipping point for phosphate produced in Florida.

Old world elegance in Tampa

After Henry Plant built his fabulous Tampa Bay Hotel, he and his wife toured Europe to find just the right furnishings for it. What they brought home gave the hotel an elegant style unmatched in Florida up to that time. There were Florentine mirrors, and carpets that had been created for British royalty. Plant even bought rickshaws to carry his guests up and down the long halls so that they would not tire.

The pictures above, taken in the Plant Museum, offer an example of the showplace he constructed to provide luxury quarters at the Tampa railroad terminal to encourage greater travel to Florida's west coast, then a frontier-like area.

Ybor City, the Cuban quarter in Tampa where the cigar makers from Key West first settled, includes such Spanish restaurants as the one pictured at right, where both the food and the atmosphere are authentic. They have become famous statewide.

Tampa Bay:
the highest bridge
in Florida

*The Sunshine Skyway
puts a gateway across Tampa
Bay from St. Petersburg
toward Bradenton and Sarasota to the south.
So that ships entering and
leaving Tampa's
busy port may pass freely,
the bridge was built
with the highest elevation of
any in Florida.
Fishermen take advantage
of its long, low
approaches to try their luck
with both pier and
surf casting, or handlines.*

On central Florida's other coast, activity centers around Tampa Bay. Clustered near the bay are Tampa, St. Petersburg, Clearwater and, not far to the south, Bradenton and Sarasota. Like Miami, Tampa's large Spanish language population makes it bilingual. The city juts out into Tampa Bay and its port stays busy as a distribution center. Tampa's international Airport is the most modern in Florida. In addition to the cigar-makers of Ybor City, Tampa's economy turns on MacDill Air Force Base, phosphate, beer, tourism, seafood, citrus, beef, vegetables, and manufacturing of such items as computers and air conditioning units.

But the story of Tampa, of course, revolves around Henry Plant and it is easier to appreciate both if you visit his old Tampa Bay Hotel. A quarter-century after the Civil War, Plant bought 60 acres along the Hillsborough River for $40,000. Then he spent $3 million building and furnishing the elegant Moorish-Turkish hotel with 13 minarets. Plant's railroad, which virtually created Tampa, ran past the hotel to Tampa Bay. At night, bonfires lighted the lawns of the hotel so the train passengers could not fail to see it. Plant once ran rickshaws up and down the long halls so that his heavily walleted guests would not tire too quickly in their pleasures. In 1905, Plant's heirs sold the hotel to the city for $125,000 and 27 years later (during the Depression) the University of Tampa leased it for one dollar per year. Now the university and the city maintain one wing of the hotel as the Henry B. Plant Museum, which preserves the prized furnishings he imported from Europe.

The Spanish flavor of Tampa centers around Ybor City, the area purchased by Vicente Martinez Ybor in 1886 and into which he moved his cigar factories. In 1869, Ybor had fled Cuba to Key West, a refugee from oppression by Spanish troops (Cuba then was a Spanish colony). He moved to Tampa after labor disputes became disruptive and fire destroyed some of his factories. Ybor City survives today as a Cuban Quarter.

The 186-acre Busch Gardens, a wild animal compound created with the look of an African Veldt, draws many visitors, as does the annual Gasparilla pirate invasion. The city adopted the pirate Jose Gaspar as a rogue patron and each February holds a festival recreating his legendary invasion.

Tampa's twin city on the bay, St. Petersburg, was founded in 1876 as a tourist resort. A Russian exile named it for his hometown. St. Petersburg has Florida's highest bridge (the Sunshine Skyway over the mouth of Tampa Bay with a clearance of 150.5 feet), may have had the first Chamber of Commerce with a promotion budget, and has an undeserved reputation as a city of old folk. In 1902, the chamber doled out $150 to promote

147

At night, the twin cities of St. Petersburg and Tampa put a sparkle of light all around Tampa Bay. Here, reflections from St. Petersburg's waterfront buildings join a soft, distant glow on the horizon for a pleasing effect. The city was founded as a tourist resort.

When sun goes down, St. Petersburg lights up

St. Petersburg, once known as a city of the elderly, now can haul out statistics to show you that in fact the young outnumber the senior citizens. However, as the Chamber of Commerce points out, almost anyone would like it in this sunny, coastal city where boating and swimming and fishing and the outdoors life are a basic ingredient. For the less athletic there are lots of benches. Growth here is one reason why Florida bulges in the middle, with no diet in sight.

The Bounty: for fun and cameras

H. M. S. Bounty, replica of the old sailing ship, docks at St. Petersburg's pier, and children escort their parents aboard for an enthusiastic tour. The cannon, the rigging and masts make it a prime picture subject. In this climate, it is not hard to imagine the Bounty again sailing the South Seas.

These days the Bounty flies the U.S. flag, and her mission neither brooks nor risks a mutiny. It's all for fun. Nobody mutinies.

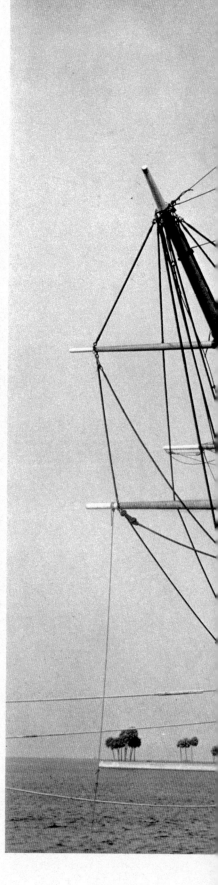

the city and kill rumors of a smallpox epidemic. If that was not the first such Florida effort, certainly it was quite early among the first. The benign climate and salt-air breezes that made tourism an anchor of the economy brought many of those tourists back as retirees, especially during the 1950's. However, statistics show the young outnumber the old.

Like other Sun Coast cities, St. Petersburg features the outdoors life – boating, swimming, fishing, or just walking in the many parks. It claims the world's most unusual drugstore, Webb's City, a conglomeration of all kinds of shops from gas stations to supermarkets to pharmacies. Major league baseball teams have trained here since 1914. They were not the first, though. Jacksonville holds that honor. The old Washington Nationals set the pattern by coming to Jacksonville in the spring of 1885.

Above St. Petersburg, the city of Clearwater, with the same outdoors emphasis, flourishes on tourism. Across the Sunshine Skyway south, Bradenton, Sarasota and the resort keys (Lido, St. Armand's and Bradenton's Anna Maria Island) follow in quick order. Bradenton, which asserts that Hernando DeSoto first set foot in Florida nearby, commemorates that event each year with a costumed festival depicting his arrival. Sarasota, known as a city of culture, owes much of its charm and even affluence to its pioneer benefactors, John Ringling, the circus king and oil magnate, and Mrs. Potter Palmer, the onetime "Queen of Chicago." Ringling made Sarasota the winter home of his circus (now 15 miles south in Venice), and left behind a complex known as the Ringling Museums which helped put the city on its cultural bent. The complex includes his Venetian-style mansion on the bay (built in 1925 at a cost of $1.5 million), the John and Mable Ringling Museum of Art, the Museum of the Circus and the Asolo Theater. The art museum has an extensive collection of the paintings of Rubens, the Flemish master. Florida purchased the Asolo Theater, built in Italy in 1798, in 1950 and moved it to the Ringling estate. It serves as the State Theater of Florida. Mrs. Palmer, a widow and national celebrity at the time, caused a stir by announcing that she considered Sarasota Bay among the world's most beautiful places. Then she set about buying (about 1911) 140,000 acres of land at a time when land was not in demand. Her energy, faith, influence and money made a difference. At Osprey, she chose as her home a 213-acre estate called The Oaks. She invested successfully in citrus groves and cattle, as a rancher introducing dipping vats to rid cattle of ticks, bringing in the Brahma strain (it was resistant to ticks), fencing up her purebred stock and shipping the first full trainload of cattle to, of all places, Texas.

151

When Walt Disney
World came to Florida,
the impact changed many
of the accepted rules
of tourism. So great was the
attraction that it
caused a major shift in the
flow of tourist traffic.
The Disney characters, and
the appeal of the
environment created for
their showcase,
brought a series of satellite
attractions that
may make Orlando and
central Florida
the new tourism center.
Disney started it all.

Cinderella and Mickey Mouse live here

152

Edison found Fort Myers the ideal winter home

Thomas A. Edison, who invented the electric light bulb, established a home and experimental laboratory in Fort Myers, where he spent each winter for some 40 years. "There is only one Fort Myers," he would say, and predicted that one day millions would agree with him. The picture below shows the laboratory where he worked.

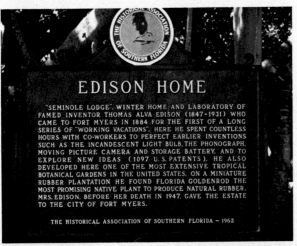

EDISON HOME

"SEMINOLE LODGE", WINTER HOME AND LABORATORY OF FAMED INVENTOR THOMAS ALVA EDISON (1847-1931) WHO CAME TO FORT MYERS IN 1884 FOR THE FIRST OF A LONG SERIES OF "WORKING VACATIONS". HERE HE SPENT COUNTLESS HOURS WITH CO-WORKERS TO PERFECT EARLIER INVENTIONS SUCH AS THE INCANDESCENT LIGHT BULB, THE PHONOGRAPH, MOVING PICTURE CAMERA AND STORAGE BATTERY, AND TO EXPLORE NEW IDEAS (1097 U.S. PATENTS). HE ALSO DEVELOPED HERE ONE OF THE MOST EXTENSIVE TROPICAL BOTANICAL GARDENS IN THE UNITED STATES. ON A MINIATURE RUBBER PLANTATION HE FOUND FLORIDA GOLDENROD THE MOST PROMISING NATIVE PLANT TO PRODUCE NATURAL RUBBER. MRS. EDISON, BEFORE HER DEATH IN 1947, GAVE THE ESTATE TO THE CITY OF FORT MYERS.

THE HISTORICAL ASSOCIATION OF SOUTHERN FLORIDA – 1962

Among Edison's friends and sponsors, one who came to Fort Myers because of him was Henry Ford. In the Edison museum, now owned and operated by the city of Fort Myers and open to the public, are a Ford given him by the automobile manufacturer, some of Edison's early phonographs, and scientific exhibits.

TIRE MADE FROM GOLDEN-ROD RUBBER FORMERLY ON EDISON'S MODEL T FORD

EDISON'S MODEL 'T' FORD PRESENTED TO HIM BY HIS FRIEND~NEIGHBOR HENRY FORD

In his Fort Myers laboratory, Edison invented synthetic rubber made of the goldenrod blooms.

Cypress Gardens: pretty girls make an art of skiing

At Cypress Gardens, which gets its name from the ancient trees that grow along the shoreline, the combination of pretty girls and unusual skill on water skis has made it a popular stopping place for Florida visitors. The natural

beauty of the place and the color created by its water shows manage to offer a touch of old Florida at the same time they display the new. The cypress tree, found around many of Florida's lakes and rivers, has come to symbolize for some the beautiful natural setting that existed long before Ponce de Leon landed. Cypress Gardens formalizes a scene that is distinctly Florida. At left, the girls ski in formation. Above, visitors study the cypress stands from a tour boat.

157

Oranges get ripe in the fall, and harvesters don long sacks and spread through the groves to pick them. They are paid for the boxes they can fill.

Oranges and other citrus fruits grow throughout Florida, but the greatest number come out of the central part of the state, where they can be relatively safe from frost as well as the tropical humidity. The ridge, a high hump of land running up the middle of the state, and the Indian River are two famous producing areas. One Florida county, Polk, grows more oranges than does all of California. At the extreme right, a closeup view of oranges still on the tree.

Along Florida's
ridge, oranges
grow by millions

160

In the 1960's, men began to build space ships

When John F. Kennedy was elected president, he promised that Americans would fly to the moon and return safely. At the time, it appeared impossible. Yet within a decade, not only that promise was fulfilled, but many others. The Kennedy Space Center at Cape Canaveral became the site of some of America's most inspirational achievements. At left, the camera catches a missile as its rockets belch flame and it begins to lift off the launching pad. At right, Dr. Kurt Debus, director of the space center, at his desk. The picture below illustrates the docking operation in space as planned for the first joint U.S.-Soviet Union test project.

In one brief stretch above Tampa Bay, three cities still pay homage to their Old World beginnings. Dunedin, just north of Clearwater on the coast, was founded as Jonesboro but two Scotsmen came along in 1882 and changed it to Dunedin, Gaelic for Edinburgh, their former home. Dunedin holds an annual Highland Games and Festival, with kilted bagpipers and dancing. A little farther up the road, the better known Tarpon Springs keeps alive a Greek heritage. Greek sponge fishermen migrated here from Key West around 1905 and they still search for and market the golden zoofiton (Greek for sponge). Tarpon Springs, incidentally, is not one of those famous Florida bubbling springs. The name, according to oldtimers, began when someone saw the flash of fish in the water and exclaimed, "The tarpon springs." Out of the expression grew the name. Less wellknown is Masaryktown, on U.S. 41. During the Boom, in 1924, a group of Czechoslovakians from New York founded the town with a vision of making it the largest in Florida. Thomas Masaryk, the namesake, was a Czech independence hero. The town is smaller than when founded, but holds an annual festival at which Czech costumes, dancing and cooking may be appreciated by the public.

Florida's famous springs begin to appear on the upper gulf coast of central Florida. Weekiwachee, Homosassa and Crystal River have become tourist attractions largely on the basis of the springs and the waters that flow from them. Weekiwachee and Homosassa both are first magnitude springs, which means they are among the 17 strongest in Florida and the 75 strongest in all of the United States. A first magnitude spring gushes at least 64.6 million gallons of water daily. The waters from several springs form Crystal River, around which a community developed that has become wellknown both to sportsmen and to fanciers of seafood.

Typical of the small, inland central Florida towns are Brooksville (on U.S. 41) and Dade City (on U.S. 301), both northeast of Tampa but west of Orlando. The climate stays mostly gentle in this agricultural area, so that the oranges can grow and the cattle can feed and the tourists won't turn sour. Occasionally, winter threatens enough to make the grumpy be thankful, and to provide sweet touches of fall and spring, when zest can overcome worry. Citrus groves make dark buffers between the cattle ranches and the farms, breaking up smooth fields and pastures, ending long furrows that run across the hills in pin-stripes. Brooksville holds an annual Dogwood Festival and Dade City a Heart of Florida Folk Festival. The nearby community of San Antonio has an annual rattlesnake roundup.

Oranges grow in more than half of Florida's 67 counties, but their commercial growth is con-

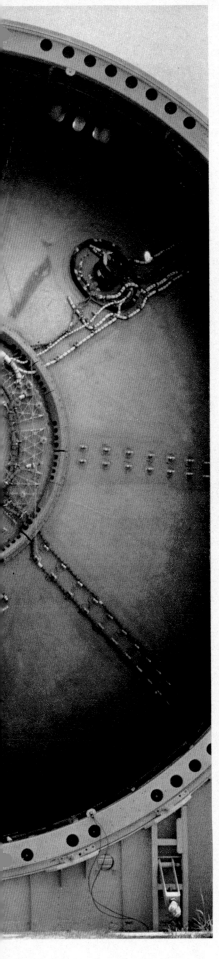

The relics of the rocket age at the Kennedy Space Center are hardly older than the youngsters who flock there daily for the bus tours and exhibits which tell the story of America's journeys to the moon, and of the beginning of its current efforts to create the revolutionary new Space Shuttle. The shuttle will combine the advantages of airplanes and spaceships, making it possible to fly the same craft repeatedly into space and back to earth. Scientists say the shuttle will make space flight more simple, shorter, less expensive and more clearly practical in its benefits to earth.

The cape: from space frontier to museum

At Daytona Beach, where automobile racing got its start on the sandy shore, the annual "Firecracker 400" race i

...ne of the major events. Here, the cars flash around the banked speedway turns as fans watch from a crowded infield.

A motorbike caravan parades single-file along the sands at Daytona Beach, called the World's Most Famous Beach. The broad, white sands offer an excellent driving surface. Some even pitch tents. Here the Broadwalk with its carnival atmosphere, plus the many oceanfront motels and hotels, create a lively scene especially attractive to the young. At

lower left, a long shot down the beach shows the surf and sand, where a thick line of cars marks the water's edge. Spring, summer and fall are the seasons here, but it's busy all year.

On Daytona Beach, a carnival of fun

Middle Florida, where there's enough chill to sweeten fall

In central Florida, where Disney World has made Orlando a visitors' hub, there's a little of both the north and the south mixed for a pleasing range of Florida delights. In the picture at left, a barking dog hails a sailboat zipping along the Atlantic Ocean near Titusville, as bathers soak up the sun in comfort. East coast beaches such as these are less wellknown than those along the Gold Coast, but also less crowded and equally appealing during the warmer months. At right, a shot of Orlando, a city of lakes and parks, and the largest in Florida not touching on either the ocean or the gulf. Major highways intersect at Orlando and make it a natural crossroads in Florida, easily accessible to many of the state's attractions.

169

Sarasota: the circus brought it museums

John Ringling, circus owner and oil magnate, made Sarasota his home and he left it a cultural heritage that few Florida cities can match. Ringling's contributions, some shown here, included his home built in 1925, the Ringling Museum of Art and the Museum of the Circus. Sarasota, south of Tampa Bay, enjoyed numerous other contributions to its cultural life, including the Italian Asolo Theater.

Sarasota, perhaps because of the Ringling influence, always has enjoyed a varied and unusual range of cultural activities. In later years, it has become a favorite gathering place as well as permanent home for a number of well-known artists and writers. Nearby islands, such as Lido and St. Armand's, have added to the reputation of Sarasota as a resort and home for the well-to-do. Mrs. Potter Palmer of Chicago brought Sarasota national attention during the early years of its development.

centrated among the endless lakes of central Florida and near the highlands or ridge section. Florida produces about two-thirds of the U.S. citrus and Polk County alone, as one example, produces more than the entire state of California. Migrant labor, attracted to Florida by the range of seasonal work in south Florida's winter vegetable and sugarcane farms, begins harvesting the citrus crops in late fall.

Lakeland, largest city in Polk County and home of the Florida Citrus Commission and Florida Southern College (some of its buildings designed by the architect Frank Lloyd Wright), thrives on citrus, phosphate and tourism. Florida accounts for one-third of the world's supply of phosphate and most of Florida's production comes out of Polk, but there is phosphate in Hillsborough, Manatee and Hardee counties, too. While citrus generally adds to the beauty and charm of this area, the phosphate industry faces the problems of dealing with air and water pollution, land reclamation and the issue of a fair tax load. In his book, The Florida Phosphate Industry, Arch Fredric Blakey concludes that resolution of these problems involves a more realistic management of American values. But he says Florida has dominated this vital industry since the beginning of the century, and with its abundant supply probably will continue to do so. Clustering near Lakeland are Bartow and the little town of Mulberry, where the phosphate industry controls the scene; Plant City, a strawberry center named for Henry Plant; and Winter Haven, made famous by the water-skiing bathing beauties at lovely Cypress Gardens.

A stretch of U.S. 27 from Leesburg south through Clermont, Haines City, Lake Wales, Frostproof, Avon Park and Sebring, must be included among Florida's most scenic. This includes the elevated ridge section and has hills, lakes and citrus groves in abundance. Leesburg — and a cluster of towns just east of it that includes Tavares, Eustis and Mount Dora — are heavily involved in the citrus industry. They are small, picturesque places with distinct personalities. Leesburg, founded in 1853 by the Lee family of New York, is geared to agriculture, sometimes is called Florida's watermelon capital and asserts claim — one which several Florida cities contest — to the best bass fishing lakes. Mount Dora, rising off the shores of Lake Dora, was laid out in 1882 with lawns and streets in the style of a New England village. Canals connecting Lake Dora and others make it possible for boaters to reach the Oklawaha River, the St. Johns River and the Atlantic Ocean.

From two towers along U.S. 27, the Citrus Tower (200 feet) at Clermont and Lake Placid Tower (240 feet) at Lake Placid, there are spectacular views of the countryside. Between the two along that same highway are Haines City, named

171

Ranches: still a kingdom for a horse

Beneath a moss-bearded oak, horses graze in a pasture near Arcadia, part of Florida's cattle country. While mechanized travel has put the horse out of the transportation business generally, it remains an important factor in ranch life. No wheeled machines yet have been able to know and respond to their masters or precisely wheel and herd a cow, in the way a horse can. Above, ranch hands in broad-brimmed hats, with ropes on their saddles, provide a scene that at first glance might appear to be more Western than Floridian. But cattle rank among the major industries in Florida.

for Henry Plant's righthand man (and engineer), Col. Henry S. Haines; Lake Wales, a jewel among Florida's cities; Frostproof, a citrus community given its name by oldtimers who insisted cold weather would slide off the slopes of the ridge and leave the town frostproof; Avon Park, named for William Shakespeare's Stratford-on-Avon; and Sebring, home of the annual International Grand Prix Sports Car race.

Downtown Lake Wales has been converted into a shoppers' mall. Nearby are Masterpiece Gardens and the Black Hills Passion play, as well as Spook Hill, where the young find delight in watching cars apparently roll uphill rather than down. But the major fascination probably is Bok Tower at the 128-acre Mountain Lake Sanctuary atop Iron Mountain, one of the highest points (324 feet) in Florida. The tower was the inspiration of Edward W. Bok, noted magazine editor and Pulitzer Prize winning author, who called it "America's Taj Mahal." Bok dedicated the sanctuary and the tower to the American people as a retreat of natural beauty, a place of meditation. The Singing Tower has a 53-bell carillon which gives daily recitals.

Though there are large cattle ranches southward in the areas around Lake Okeechobee, central Florida can lay claim to being cattle headquarters. Both Kissimmee, south of Orlando, and Arcadia, 45 miles west of Sarasota, are major cattle towns and hold annual rodeos, but ranches are scattered across the area. One of Florida's largest is Deseret, owned by the Mormon Church (Church of Jesus Christ of Latter Day Saints), which covers 300,000 acres of Florida between Orlando and the east coast near St. Cloud. The ranch, purchased by the church in 1950, measures roughly 50 miles long and 30 miles wide.

Cattle ranching among the palms, instead of cactus or mesquite, may seem a little out of kilter but Florida has been raising cattle longer than any other state. Ponce de Leon brought them here on his second trip in 1521. The industry got a boost during the Civil War when the Yankee blockade cut off the Confederacy from Texas cattle. Florida was able to drive its cattle herds up from the southern prairies to the railheads near Jacksonville where they could be shipped into Georgia. The state's wartime salt works industry, which sprang up partly because salt was the best means of preserving beef, helped the cause. After the war, during Reconstruction, the cattle roamed freely and Florida became known as the home of the "scrub" cow. In later years, as the ranches turned to better strains (Brahmas, Angus, Herefords, Santa Gertrudis, Charolais), both the reputation and the beef improved.

One of the most colorful men in the state's history was the Cracker cowboy, Florida's version of the legendary Western cowboy. But there was

Real, live Cracker cowboys still ride range in Florida

There's no mesquite or tumbleweed for the cowboys to sing about in Florida, but they have all the cows they can handle. The south central flatlands are the prairies. Pine and palm and a two-rut road make up the scene as these cowboys at Rainbow Ranch near Myakka City drive a herd to pasture. The cattle industry began to grow importantly during the Civil War when Florida supplied the South's beef.

The most popular legend about Cracker cowboys grew around an unlikely fellow named Bone Mizell, who worked for ranches near Arcadia. A plaque in his memory has been erected along the Peace River at Zolfo Springs. Most tales of Bone Mizell spring from his powerful thirst, and the unhappy situations this brought upon him. In history, he may prove to be Florida's best known, if not most typical, cowboy.

Bok Tower: most serene spot in Florida

In all of Florida, the Bok Tower probably rates as the most serene, inspirational public gathering place. Located on Iron Mountain near Lake Wales, the tower was created for the sole purpose of providing beauty and repose. In the picture (at right on the facing page), the carillon tower and reflecting pool are shown. The carillon plays daily recitals. The sanctuary's gardens and grounds are home to many birds and squirrels, which will feed from your hand. The picture on the lefthand page shows an example of the tropical banyan-type tree and its speading root system.

a difference. Frederic Remington, the cowboy artist, came to Florida to make comparisons and was disappointed. The Florida "cattle hunters" rarely used a rope and hardly ever a sixgun. Remington could find few overtones of knighthood either in their dress or behavior. He wrote once that they were "wild-looking individuals, whose hanging hair and drooping hats and generally bedraggled appearance would remind you at once of the Spanish moss . . ." With such criticism, Remington discouraged the making of any romantic legends about the Cracker Cowboy, but some unromantic ones have managed to spring up. Many of these center around the character of an unlikely fellow named Napoleon Bonepart Mizell, better known as Bone. He was from an old town called Pine Level near Arcadia but the Peace River Valley Historical Society at its museum near Zolfo Springs has erected a plaque memorializing him.

The tales of Bone Mizell are endless, and all worthwhile as examples of Florida folklore. Many believe Bone met Frederic Remington and was responsible for the artist's disappointments. Mizell, described as wheezing, lisping, and hook-nosed, became known for getting drunk on moonshine and sobering up on lemon extract. According to legend, Mizell rode his horse into Tampa saloons and drank at the bar while sitting in the saddle; when drunk enough, would light his pipe with dollar bills; once won a bet by branding a stray steer with his teeth; rustled cattle routinely and, all the while, lived and spoke so outrageously that he became both the horror and delight of his community, depending upon its good humor at the time. When Mizell died in 1921, the death certificate listed "moonshine" as the cause.

Once, a wealthy New England family asked Mizell to dig up the body of their son, who had died of malaria while trying to be a cowboy. Mizell, who knew the boy, discovered he was buried next to an old Cracker who had never been out of Florida. So Mizell shipped the bones of the old Cracker up North, satisfied that the boy would not have wanted to go back and that the oldtimer would be happy at getting a chance to travel. Another time, after Mizell passed out drinking moonshine, some friends decided to play a joke on him. They carried him to a cemetery and laid him out in a coffin. Then they circled him with pine knots, set them afire, and waited to see what would happen when he awakened. After awhile, Bone raised up, blinking. He looked around at the tombstones and drawled, "Wal, here it is jedgment day and I'm the fust one up."

Considering all that is packed into central Florida, lakes and oranges and Mickey Mouse and astronauts sandwiched between splendid beaches and the attentive sun, it is easy to understand why the state has developed a bulging middle.

177

Breakers roll in on the east coast, make good surfing

On the upper east coast, especially around Daytona, the broad, flat beaches encourage the kind of long, rolling wave that surfers love. In these pictures, taken near Daytona, surfers demonstrate how – and how not to – catch the curve of a breaker and ride into shore just ahead of its boiling, foamy power.

The Historic North

The first part of Florida discovered and settled was the last to feel the explosive growth. North Florida, where the early struggles of state history took place, still resembles in patches the land that the old Crackers loved so much. They provide striking counterpoint to the cities. While all of Florida is marked by sharp contrasts, perhaps here in the historic north they are greatest.

The largest urban area is Jacksonville, which adopted the slogan The Bold New City of the South. The most graceful is Tallahassee, the capital. Out across the Panhandle, Pensacola argues that it really should be called the oldest.

North Florida is so different that it could be another state. Exotic plants and shrubs are replaced by hardier species. There are magnolias instead of orchids. A few low hills roll up and add softness to the landscape. Houses are built to handle sudden rushes of cold in the winter as well as to let in the light and air when the cold just as suddenly goes away. North Florida has a priceless, captivating variety. It is like neither the magical south nor the bulging middle, but special and different.

On the northeast coast, from Fernandina Beach down to St. Augustine, much of Florida's early history occurred. A 'long sweep of salt marshes and the Amelia River separate Fernandina Beach, a quaint island fishing village, from the mainland. The smell of the sea is strong. Tidal water creeps high into marsh grasses and when it recedes the mud flats seem to rise.

In a historical sense, Fernandina Beach itself has followed a cycle of rise and fall. At times its citizens have been awash with good fortune, and at others that has flowed away and left the town struggling on the flats. Since the Frenchman Jean Ribault discovered Amelia Island in 1562, eight flags (including the French) have flown over Fernandina Beach. All manner of men, from pirates to statesmen, have made it their headquarters.

War, yellow fever epidemics, hurricanes and the Depression have wiped out one boom after another and each time there has been a rebirth. At various times it has been hailed as a fig culture center, a silk center and the New York of the South. None of these things ever happened. It has settled down to a fishing village, pulp mills, tourists and a resort development which bears the island's name. It has a saloon, with hand-carved bar, built in 1878; a 100-year-old train depot; a section of remarkable 19th century homes, one made of tabby (similar to coquina); Fort Clinch (built in 1847) State Park for history buffs, beachcombers and campers.

The Buccaneer Trail (Highway AIA) goes south out of Fernandina Beach through Little Talbot Island State Park (beaches and dunes in their natural state) to Fort George Island at the mouth of the St. Johns River. There, the state has preserved a 1200-acre plantation that once belonged to a strongminded Scotsman named Zephaniah Kingsley. He was a slave trader with a sympathy for slaves (he married one), gentleman farmer and merchant king and lived on the plantation for several years beginning in 1813. In his will, bequeathing a major share of his estate to his African wife, Kingsley noted that he was of sound mind and "it is not anybody's damn business what I do with it . . . ."

A car ferry runs a regular daily schedule across the St. Johns River to Mayport, a fishing village which draws its name from the fact that Jean Ribault called this the River of May. A1A continues past the U.S. naval base at Mayport, through the Jacksonville Beaches and Ponte Vedra to the single most historic city in all of Florida, St. Augustine.

Much of what Pedro Menendez wrought there has been recreated. The old fort, Castillo de San Marcos, remains a landmark. The state has restored the old quarter (called San Agustin An-

Tallahassee, the capital, graceful city of trees

In Tallahassee, the capital of Florida, more trees are planted than are cut down. It is a city that loves to remember the genteel ways and the columned mansions of the Old South at the same time that it accommodates explosive growth. The heat and light of law-making, and the functioning of state government, assure Tallahassee both ferment and continuing change.

Florida Gov. Reubin Askew, at left, stands in front of his official residence in Tallahassee, called the Governor's Mansion. In the picture below him, a visiting school choir rests on the steps of the Capitol. At right, a full view of the building, with historic dome and cupola. Tallahassee became the capital in a historic compromise between Pensacola and St. Augustine.

183

Where laws are made, and unmade

Above, an inside look into the chamber of the Florida Senate, upper house in the state's bicameral system of legislature. Here, the process of lawmaking reaches its final stages. The picture at lower right shows students walking across the campus of Florida State University, one of the oldest and largest in the state.

tiguo) into approximately what it was in the time of the Spanish. There seems to be an endless number of other places of tourist and historical interest, but none to compare with the fort and the old city. A visitors information center shows films and passes out literature. The easiest way to see the highlights is aboard horsedrawn carriages and tour trains which make regular circuits of the town, with knowledgeable guides pointing out the possibilities. Among these is the first hotel that Henry Flagler built in Florida, the magnificent old Ponce de Leon, now used by Flagler College. St. Augustine presents The Cross and Sword, a musical drama depicting the founding of St. Augustine and adopted as an official Florida play, each summer.

The story of the largest city in north Florida, and one of the most important in the state, reflects the drama in Florida's mainstream of history. Originally Jacksonville began at a bend in the St. Johns River, about 15 miles from the Atlantic Ocean. The Timucua Indians had named this point, where the river narrowed and there were firm, sloping banks, Wacca Pilatka, or the place where the cows crossed. Later the Spanish translated that to El Vado de Las Vacas. When the English and Americans came along, they called it Cow Ford. Jacksonville extended its city limits in 1967, and now the city reaches along both sides of the river all the way to the ocean. Covering an area of 766 square miles, it ranks among America's largest in land area.

Isaiah D. Hart founded Jacksonville in 1821 when he moved down from St. Marys, Ga., and traded $72 worth of cattle for 200 acres. There he laid out the city, which was incorporated in 1822.

Jacksonville did not begin to assume importance until the Civil War, when population tripled to more than 6,000 between 1860 and 1870. Steamboats had begun to run up and down the river in 1831, but St. Augustine, Pensacola and Key West then were Florida's big cities. An 1854 fire, followed by a yellow fever epidemic three years later, helped keep the lid on. Between 1870 and 1880, when the rest of the country began discovering Florida weather, Jacksonville caught the tourist traffic because this was where the transportation stopped. Jacksonville then called itself "The Winter City in Summerland." Some of the Swells floated on down the river toward such health spas as Green Cove Springs, where there were good accommodations and the spring water was considered medicinal, and Palatka, a shipping supply center for area settlers.

Jacksonville's greatest disaster occurred in 1901, just as it was reaching status as a transportation, financial and manufacturing center. A fiber plant caught fire downtown and swept through 466 acres, including 2,400 frame buildings and

Above, a picture taken inside the state House of Representatives, known as the lower house in the legislature. The men seated at the desks are elected on a proportional basis from counties throughout Florida. In theory, they represent a composite of the state, passing laws that reflect and sum up Florida attitudes.

185

Panama City: wind rises and sailors get ready

Sailors, swimmers and just plain sunbathers swarm to Panama City's beaches during the warm months. From Georgia and Alabama, it's only a short drive across Florida's Panhandle to the Miracle Strip and some of the state's nicest coastline. The unusually fine sand and clear water provide exceptional recreation, even in a state renowned for its good beaches. In the picture at left, rental sailboats are taken up fast when the wind rises. At right, some less adventure – some visitors prefer chair and umbrella to exercise and sunburn.

A time to ride, to eat, and to play

If the children get tired of the sand and water at Panama City, the huge amusement park awaits them with an almost endless variety of thrill rides, goofy games and also such exotic food items as cotton candy, hot dogs, popcorn and ice cream. If it seems old to you, then maybe you're getting old. But here among these very young the enchantment remains as fresh and exciting as it was last summer, and probably will stay that way for at least one or two more. At Panama City, parents at least do not need to worry about how they shall keep the young ones entertained. Either on the beach or at the amusement park, almost any child can find a way to stay busy.

188

Panama City's reputation as the playground of the Panhandle stems partially from the lure of this huge amusement park. Its bright lights and loud music sometime seem enough to be seen and maybe heard all the way up to the Georgia and Alabama borders. It furnishes in the traditional way what many in north Florida grew up believing should be expected of any family vacation taken at one of Florida's beaches and carnival boardwalks.

nearly all the city. That was the city's first rebuilding job. During the 1950's and the 1960's, Jacksonville revitalized its downtown with a riverfront beautification and civic development effort that became a model for other cities. Its government buildings, bridges and riverside skyscrapers give it one of Florida's most impressive skylines. Jacksonville has become an insurance center and an industrialized city, with a diversification that includes shipyards, pulp and paper products, cigars and chemical products. The busy seaport, international airport and the Jacksonville Naval Air Station (in addition to the Mayport base) add to the economic base.

The Indians called the St. Johns River the Welaka (now the name of an interesting town along its banks above Lake George), which meant River of Lakes. It rises from a swampy area west of the Indian River in central Florida, and flows north 273 miles to the Atlantic Ocean. It passes through lake after lake, the largest of which is 70-square-mile Lake George. At the northern end of the lake, on Drayton Island, Zephaniah Kingsley once had another plantation and raised oranges.

In 1828, Congress began consideration of a canal across north Florida so that ships would not have to sail all the way around the fat finger to reach gulf coast cities, including New Orleans at the mouth of the Mississippi River. The reasoning was that it not only would shorten the distances involved, but would provide ships greater security from pirates or from an enemy in time of war. More than 100 years later, in the 1930's, work went ahead briefly on a project to link the St. Johns and Oklawaha Rivers and cut across the state to the Withlacoochee River and into the Gulf of Mexico at Yankeetown. Work began again in 1964 and stopped again in 1971. Environmentalists, arguing that the canal would do irreparable damage to natural beauty along the route (particularly the Oklawaha) and questioning the value of the canal itself, mustered enough political support to make it doubtful whether the ancient dream ever would be realized.

Between the St. Johns and the Suwannee Rivers are the cities of Gainesville and Ocala, the history of which date back to DeSoto. They represent, in many ways, the heartland of Florida. Explorers, Indians and early settlers crossed paths and purposes here. Gainesville got its start in 1830 as a trading post called Hog Town and later was named for Edmund P. Gaines, a general in the Second Seminole War. Gainesville revolves around the University of Florida, which began as a private school in Ocala in 1853 called the East Florida Seminary, and was moved into Gainesville after the Civil War. A broad belt of low, sandy hills and hundreds of lakes flank the city on the east. Such places as Melrose and Keystone Heights, because of the lakes, have become favored

Pier group watches the water sports

All you really need to enjoy the gulf waters and beaches is a little energy and the opportunity. Here, the group on this pier near Panama City lacks only the opportunity as it enviously watches some more fortunate lads frolic (in the picture upper left) on a pair of air mattresses. Lower right, below the pier, a tiny sailboat illustrates a slightly more sophisticated approach to play, but there's hardly a measurable difference in the amount of pleasure gained, except for those on the pier.

homes for commuters. Toward the south are picturesque Micanopy, named for the Seminole chief, and a number of quiet towns in or near the Orange and Lochloosa lakes, including Cross Creek, once the home of Pulitzer Prize winning novelist (for The Yearling) Marjorie Kinnan Rawlings. Her old, shingle-roofed frame Cracker home, willed to the University of Florida, is maintained as a museum.

Mrs. Rawlings moved to these backwoods, called the Big Scrub country, in 1928 from a newspaper job in New York. Within a few years, she became the greatest spokesman for the "gentle, honest" Cracker, usually a poor backwoods farmer descended from migrants who left homes in Georgia, Alabama and the Carolinas. Some historians insist that the term Cracker derived from Florida cowboys who popped and cracked long buckskin whips while driving cattle. Another version is that it developed because rural Floridians cracked or pounded corn to make meal and grits, a staple of their diet. Still another story says that Cracker comes from the Spanish word Cuacaros, meaning Quakers. In his Florida Handbook, Allen Morris includes among other possibilities a 100-year-old explanation that the word Cracker began with Scottish settlers who used it to describe boastful people. Whatever the origin, for years when one Floridian spoke of another as a Cracker, it was derogatory. It raised the image of a shiftless rural Floridian. In late years, it has gained general respectability. As fewer traditional Crackers exist in modern Florida, the term has begun to mean a person who has deep roots in, and appreciations of, Florida's rural past.

In any case, Mrs. Rawlings was the first major writer to depict the Cracker sympathetically. She suggested that the ability of the oldtime Cracker to live in harmony with his environment had a certain nobility. She saw his individualistic code of conduct, which had neither moral loopholes nor elastic ethics, as a higher morality than "manmade" law. She found that the Cracker had a special attachment and sense of obligation to family.

The Big Scrub about which Mrs. Rawlings wrote was the area between Gainesville and Ocala (once Fort King) and a section east of there now dotted with white-fenced, rolling pastures of horse breeding farms. It includes the 362,000-acre Ocala National Forest, bordered on the east by the St. Johns River. Inside the forest are beautiful natural springs and lakes that make it popular with campers and outdoorsmen. Alexander Springs, Juniper Springs and Salt Springs are among the favorites. Florida's two largest springs, in terms of water flow, are privately owned but open to the public as commercial attractions. The most famous, Silver Springs near Ocala, discharges 500 million gallons of water each day. The other,

Rainbow Springs between Ocala and Yankeetown on U.S. 41 near Dunnellon, issues 450 million gallons of water daily.

Fishing villages and relatively isolated beaches dot the gulf coast from Yankeetown up to St. Marks, south of Tallahassee. There are Steinhatchee just north of the Suwannee River, the town of Suwannee at the river's mouth and Cedar Key, the most distinctive and wellknown of them all.

Late in the evening, it's quiet enough around Cedar Key to hear the splash of jumping mullet. There's not enough neon to bend around the door of one lively honky-tonk. Children stop in the street to wave at a passing car. Their elders nod and smile. Cedar Key, the town folk enjoy telling you, is more than just an isolated coastal village about halfway between Tallahassee and Tampa. They insist it is a way of life. There are no highrises, no shopping centers, no traffic to speak of, little crime and not many people. Hard times have been here often, and they threaten to return each summer between oyster and crab seasons. Most of the people here either harvest the oysters, stone crabs and blue crabs, or fish for the mullet, trout and redfish. The rest cook those delicacies to feed hungry tourists.

In 1885, Cedar Key had a population of 5,000. Now it has less than 1,000. The place boomed in 1860 when David L. Yulee's railroad ran from here to Fernandina Beach. There was not only the seafood business, but lumber mills, including cedar mills which furnished slats to pencil factories. Cedar Key was the shipping and receiving point for the area. But a combination of too intensive harvesting of both the timber and seafood resources, without thought of conservation, made them scarce. In 1896 a great hurricane and tidal wave swamped the town. Cedar Key never grew back to its former prominence.

At Suwannee, where the river flows into the gulf, the Odlund family were among the pioneers. Eric A. Odlund, a Swedish sailor, brought his 18-year-old bride. Luella Robinson, to a 10-acre island in the mouth of the Suwannee River in 1910. They built a home of scrap wood and palmetto leaves. Luella helped salt and pack the mullet so Eric could sell it down the coast at Cedar Key. She learned to make her own soap, use lanterns for light and not to fight nature. They ate turtles and fish, and vegetables from their own garden. The Odlunds raised nine children on the island, and all of them eventually settled near the river. When Eric died in 1941, at age 67, he was buried on the island in the shade of cedars beneath a Georgia granite tombstone inscribed, "King of the Suwannee".

Luella became known as Grannie Odlund, the Queen of the Suwannee. She stayed on the island, until her death in 1974. Electricity did not reach

The north: 'Old Florida' beauty

Around Lake Jackson, near Tallahassee, the special and different beauty that typifies the north Florida countryside becomes clear. There are fewer palms, more oaks, and the Spanish moss drapes over nearly every tree limb. Here, where the Florida climate is temperate rather than tropical, nature reflects the change. Most Floridians regard such scenes as typical of "Old Florida."

The swirl
of a bass,
the tug
of a bream

For the Florida fisher-man, probably no greater peace exists than that found on a lake where the only sounds are the swirl of a bass among the reeds in the shallows and the sudden whir of a spinning reel. A superb system of lakes and rivers make the state a haven for fresh-water fishermen. For those who prefer salt water, the ocean or gulf is never very far away. Here, the camera catches that special thing of the spirit that affects the sportsmen who revere the lakes. At left, on Lake Jackson, lily pads where a light-footed bird can stroll. Below, a boat skirts the reeds along the shoreline and the rod bends as a bass is reeled in. At right, a satisfied fisherman reflects on his day.

194

With umbrellas to keep the sun off, and a splendid spread of Florida lake and forest before them, these two wome

n spend a contemplative day in the countryside not far from Tallahassee and perhaps even bring home their supper

Sometimes, you must look closely

*The beauties of Florida
are not all contained in the
broad sweep of her
beaches, or the Everglades
or the magnificent
lakes. Sometimes they are
the tiny things. These,
you must stop and look
closely to see. They
cannot be fully appreciated,
and maybe not even
seen, from the window of a
passing automobile. In
these intriguing photos, a
fragile-winged insect
inspects a tip of grass pointed like a spear.
It seems a gentle world,
until you consider
that the role of an insect is
to feed upon tiny
plants and flowers, or the
smaller insects, and
then even as he rests upon
a spear like a winged,
victorious warrior, he may
be snapped up himself
in the beak of a passing bird
that is late for lunch.*

198

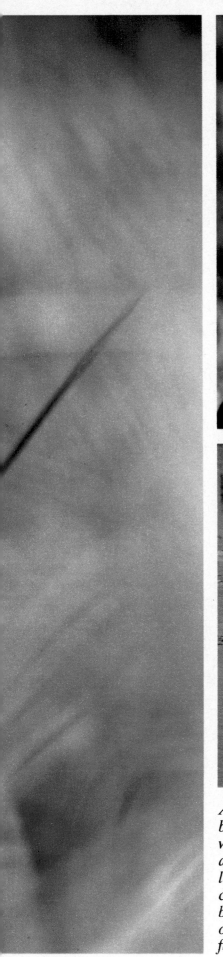

All life takes chances, even bugs, but some do it with more flair than others, adopting the philosophical line that death comes but once to the brave. In the picture above one courageous little fellow alights a top a deep purple bloom. Luckily, the bird to his right cares only for the whiff of a flower. Below, the still, neutral lake reflects the greenery it nourishes. All these are part of Florida, too, but you must look and be patient.

Families gather at rivers and lakes

Who's the best fisherman in the family? An outing on the lake or river, and discussions of the day's luck, may not ever produce a definitive answer, but it offers a convenient reason to keep coming back. At left, Dad hauls in a bass while Mother holds the net. Junior enviously watches. At right, the replica of an old steamboat cruises down the Suwannee River near Stephen Foster Memorial at White Springs. Below, another family prepares for Suwannee fishing.

The Crackers: a part of Florida's heritage

One of the most fascinating parts of Florida's history involves the rural population, who once were called Crackers. In earlier years, it was a term of derision. Now, among knowledgeable Floridians, it has become a nickname of respect from one who knows and understands what these people mean to the state in the way of a special heritage. In the pictures on these pages, the camera reveals some of those links to that Cracker past. Above, John O. Gandy (born in 1868) migrated to Florida from Alabama and now lives in a Panhandle town that bears his name. At right, Grannie Odlund until her death in 1974 was called the Queen of the Suwannee River. She was Florida born.

her home until 1953, and telephones a decade later. One afternoon in her late years, chewing snuff in the yard of the Salt Creek Baptist Church (across the creek from her island), while waiting for the missionary meeting to start, she expressed but one regret. "If we'd of had any judgment " she said, speaking of their arrival here, "we'd of bought up a whole lot of this land and we could sell it now for a good price." Practicality always was the Cracker style.

Stephen Foster's song, The Old Folks at Home, gave the Suwannee River international fame and bestowed upon it a certain mystical elegance that fit its natural beauty. Most of its people take pride in being called Crackers, and their most famous product is catfish.

The river begins in south Georgia's Okefenokee Swamp and flows across north Florida into the gulf without ever touching a town of major size. In the course of that journey it drops 35 feet closer to sea level. It curls past White Springs, a 19th century health resort and site of the state-owned Stephen Foster Memorial, and takes a parenthetical path past Ellaville, Branford and Old Town. Along the way there are occasional rapids, high stratified limestone banks, sandy bluffs, deer and other wildlife. It begins in cypress trees and ends in palm. Three other rivers and 55 springs feed into the Suwannee. Its black-looking waters actually are the color of tea, stained by tannic acid from the trees. Indians, pirates and steamboats once floated upon it and people from over the world have come here to see the river made famous by song. Oddly, Stephen Foster himself, the melancholy composer from Pennsylvania, never made it. In 1851, he was looking for a two-syllable river to use in the lyrics of a song about the South. He turned to a map and found two – the Peedee of South Carolina and the Yazoo of Mississippi. Neither fit the phrasing or the mood. He searched on, found the Suwannee (with three syllables) and dropped the middle one out – to call it Swanee.

The Suwannee meanders through good farming country, curving a few miles north of Lake City and Live Oak before making its run to the gulf. Lake City (once named Alligator, after a Seminole chief), near the Osceola National Forest, and Live Oak (named for a shade tree) sit in a tobacco growing area. Tobacco auctions are held there in August, and Live Oak stages an annual tobacco festival.

The Florida forestry industry's millions of acres in timberland scatter across north Florida, but the city of Perry calls itself The Tree Capital of the World, and therefore of Florida, too. Located 50 miles southeast of Tallahassee on U.S. 19–27, Perry has hosted an annual Florida Forest Festival since 1956 – which includes a free fish fry – and is the home of the Forest Capital State Cultural Museum, which honors the billion-dollar-plus industry.

Jacksonville, one of Florida's largest and most important cities, sits along a curve in the St. Johns River in the nort

...ast section. Here, the camera takes a view across the river in the evening, silhouetting the city's profile against the sky.

In land area, Jacksonville now is Florida's largest city and one of the largest in the entire United States. But once it was a shallow river crossing which the Indians called Cow Ford. In this aerial view, showing how the St. Johns River divides the city, the major downtown area lies to the left. It was in this city that Henry Flagler the railroad pioneer first discovered Florida's charms. The story of how Jacksonville renovated its waterfront has become a model for other cities in community development.

Jacksonville: once they called it Cow Ford

Shrimp boats stage festival at Fernandina

Fernandina Beach, on historic Amelia Island, is the place where the shrimping industry first began. The city annually reaffirms that distinction with a Shrimp Boat Festival. In the picture at far left, the fleet sweeps into the docks with flags flying. Activities include shrimp boat races, the blessing of the fleet, a demonstration of net shrimping and a parade. During its colorful history, Fernandina Beach has lived under flags of eight nationalities, and once was ruled by pirates. At the festival, local citizens set up seafood booths along the city docks and serve island specialities.

The Panhandle is another Florida, part of it old and part glistening new. The lower half, with the powdery white beaches and beautiful water, is one world; the upper half, with great open spaces and farms and pastures and Cracker beginnings, is quite another. They have opposite charms. The gracious city of Tallahassee, capital of all Florida, serves as mecca for the Panhandle.

Almost everybody loves Tallahassee at first sample. There is an old South style here that is catching. If you are not careful, pretty quick you find yourself smiling for no reason, and being randomly courteous. It is a town of hills and trees. It boasts that no significant public tree ever was cut down without a fight.

Once, it is said, the Chamber of Commerce struck a slogan for Tallahassee – "America's Next Great City". Though that was not an extravagant vision within the Florida context, it had a jarring note and was changed to "The Elegant City", which just suited. To make amends, the account continues, the Chamber exhibited the spirit of the true believer by relocating in an old white-columned mansion (the Benjamin Chaires home built in 1835) that once served as a town refuge from hostile Indians.

Tallahassee was chosen as the state capital in 1824 as a compromise between St. Augustine and Pensacola. There had been a cluster of Indian villages on the site, called Fowl Towns. The name Tallahassee comes from the Indian word meaning deserted village or abandoned fields. State government, Florida State University and Florida A & M University are the principal employers.

Before the Civil War, cities such as Monticello, Madison and Quincy set the pace for plantation life, and Tallahassee was the centerpiece. An annual festival, Springtime Tallahassee, lends special emphasis to illuminating for visitors the Tallahassee lifestyle and showing off the antebellum homes both here and nearby. This is "Where Spring Begins . . . . " they say.

Quincy, a tobacco center which has a 1913 yellowbrick courthouse with a clock tower, is boasted of in local legend as Florida's wealthiest town per capita. The story goes that a local banker around the 19th century became convinced that the soft drink Coca Cola had an unlimited future. He so advised his friends and customers, and many bought the preferred stock when it was selling for 19 cents a share. The banker was right and Quincy now lists 26 certified millionaires in its population of 8,300.

Between Tallahassee and St. Marks is Florida's deepest natural spring (185 feet), and one of the most beautiful. Wakulla Springs, privately owned but open to the public, gushes up 250 million gallons of water each day in a natural setting. The Florida Game and Freshwater Fish Commission permits no hunting in the Wakulla sanctuary, and

A more casual style of life and vacation near Fernandina

Fernandina Beach goes as far north and east as does Florida. Although the city itself is steeped with a sense of history, some of the surrounding area grew up as a weekend vacation spot and has a less formal atmosphere. At right, a dune buggy at a vacation cottage on the beach. Left, a touch of Cracker living.

Exploring the fascinating caverns of Marianna

Not often in Florida do you find any hole in the ground that does not soon fill up with water. Pleasing exceptions are the caverns at Marianna, where tourists may stroll below and explore unusual underground formations. Marianna lies west of Tallahassee in the part of Florida called the Panhandle because of the manner in which it extends over the Gulf of Mexico like a shelf, or a handle. There is no pan on the end of it, but because everyone liked the name, it became official.

Powerfully bubbling, deep springs lace Florida

Florida has more than a dozen major springs bubbling from its limestone caverns, and these spread over the central and northern parts of the state. The best known of them probably is Silver Springs near Ocala, shown in the pictures on these pages. Ocala is in north central Florida. Glass-bottomed boats, river cruises and wildlife are included among the attractions built up around the springs. There are a number of other beautiful springs which have become commercial lures to the tourist. These include Rainbow Springs near Dunnellon, Weekiwachee and Homosassa Springs along the central gulf coast. One exceptionally lovely site near Tallahassee, called Wakulla Springs, is maintained within a wildlife sanctuary in virtually a natural state.

n the pictures above, taken
t Silver Springs,
hree billygoats scramble
o suck from a baby
ottle being held up by a
mall boy. He gets
a little assistance from his
grandparents as the

goats forget their manners.
In the lower picture,
two of the glass-bottomed
boats circle above the
springs and cruise down the
Silver River, where
the clear waters and fish
charm the visitors.

uses the area and its abundant wildlife as a training camp for rangers.

The ancient city of Apalachicola, once called West Point, is located at the mouth of the Apalachicola River where it flows into the gulf. During the early 19th century, in the days of the plantations, Apalachicola and its neighboring city St. Joseph boomed. In 1838, Florida's first constitutional convention was held at St. Joseph. Bales of cotton that had been floated down the river from Georgia piled up on the docks at Apalachicola awaiting shipment to New England textile mills.

St. Joseph, known as a wicked city, for a brief period was Florida's largest. In 1841, ships brought in yellow fever and in 1845 a great hurricane rolled up a tidal wave that ended St. Joseph's 12-year life span. Both malaria and yellow fever were major problems and a brooding young physician in Apalachicola, Dr. John Gorrie, sought ways to cool the fevers of his patients. In those days, ice had to be shipped in from the Great Lakes. Dr. Gorrie's experiments led him to the invention of the first artificial ice-making machine and the first air conditioner. A museum here honors his achievements. But not many in the nation, or even Apalachicola, believed him at first.

Newspapers in the U.S. North made fun of him. "There's a crank down in Apalachicola, Florida, who claims he can make ice as good as God almighty", said one. Proof came when the ice ships did not arrive in time for the ladies' annual ice cream festival. As they wept in disappointment, Dr. Gorrie brought a home-made supply over in a wagon load of sardine cans.

Each fall as oyster season reaches its height, Apalachicola holds a seafood festival — two-thirds of the town's economy depends upon seafood — that draws 20,000 people or more to open-air Battery Park for a feast. All kinds of seafood, cooked all ways, are served while bands play and oyster-shucking and oyster-eating contests are held. It is an oldfashioned good time that grows bigger each year.

Offshore near Apalachicola are two sandy islands to which tourists flock. A ferry at Carrabelle takes cars over to Dog Island and a bridge near the mouth of the Apalachicola River links St. George Island to the mainland.

The Miracle Strip begins west of Port St. Joe (near the site of Old St. Joseph) at Panama City, and extends 100 miles to Pensacola. The name comes from the exceptionally fine beaches, and the corresponding flow of people and accommodations. The sand is unusually fine and white, and the water often so clear you can see your feet even at depths that reach your chin. The fishing, too, is good.

Panama City features a carnival area that appeals to the young. All along the strip, through beautiful Destin and its high-rises, Fort Walton Beach and on to Pensacola is the modern half of

215

216

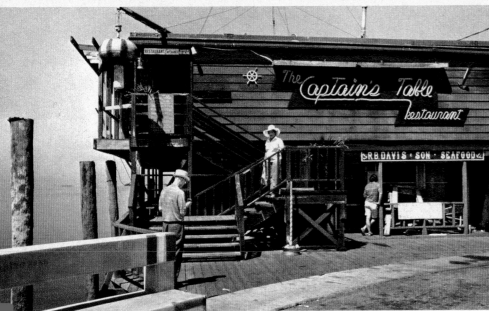

On the gulf, the pace is more deliberate

Along the upper gulf coast of Florida, between Tampa and Panama City, both the scenery and the pace of life change. There are small fishing villages, like Cedar Key (pictured above), which still live in relative isolation. There are islands and long stretches of beach which in places may look just as they did 100 years ago. The tree and wind-rippled sand dune at left are on St. George Island near Apalachicola, reached by toll bridge.

the Panhandle. It is a superb playground with parks, picnic facilities and places where you can simply park your car and step across the sand dunes for a swim. Also on or near the strip are three military bases, Eglin and Tyndall for the Air Force and Pensacola for the Navy.

Pensacola, called the City of Five Flags (Spanish, French, English, U.S. and Confederate), holds an annual Fiesta of Five Flags in the spring and An Evening in Old Seville Square in late summer. Both are oriented to history. Pensacolans say there have been more battles fought over the possession of this city than any other part of the United States. In 1967, to take advantage of its heritage, the Pensacola Historical Restoration and Preservation Commission was established as a state agency. A year later the city set aside an official Historic District which centered around old Seville Square. The street names and the buildings themselves reflect the varied Spanish, French and British influence. Additionally, a Seville Quarter has been recreated as an entertainment-restaurant complex in the same neighborhood. All of it gives Pensacola an area to compete with that of its historic rival, St. Augustine.

Old Florida resides in the upper half of the Panhandle, not as sparkling and new, but in its way just as fascinating. The town of Century, north of Pensacola near the Alabama border, was named to commemorate the founding of a sawmill in 1900. Six miles east, the farm town of Jay got new importance on the map in 1970 when a major oil strike was made. The peaceful rural scenes sprouted oil pumps and no landowner along the Panhandle could resist a bit of daydreaming as Jay began counting the new faces, the new stores and looking toward a new future.

Crestview, DeFuniak Springs, Chipley, Marianna, Blountstown and Wewahitchka are distinguished not so much by their great buildings or large industries as by their people and the quality of the lives they are able to lead. They live apart from most of the urban ills and pressures. The atmosphere of the upper Panhandle is more nearly like that of the old South than the Florida most tourists know.

Chattahoochee, settled by slaveholding plantation owners, guards the Florida entrance to the Apalachicola River. Its name comes from the Indian word meaning "three rivers." Chattahoochee is site of the Jim Woodruff Dam that forms Lake Seminole from the backwaters of three rivers flowing down from Georgia and Alabama.

The historic north is a different Florida, neither as exotic as the south nor as bulging as the middle, but anchoring the state with more traditional values and a sharper sense of history. As the old Crackers would put it, casting a suspicious glance south, north Florida is where the people have both feet firmly planted on the ground.

On special occasions, the military bands and Boy Scouts gather attention with a little pomp and circumstance, but nothing for very long overshadows the appeal of a nostalgic horse and buggy ride through the narrow streets of St. Augustine. They make a slow-motion parade through the oldest city every day, and nobody ever worries about a flat tire, or an empty gas tank.

Horse and buggy has a place in St. Augustine

Everything in the oldest city boasts of its age

The "oldest schoolhouse", shown at right, looks like a candidate for urban renewal, but that's all part of the atmosphere in St. Augustine, where the Spanish began Florida's first permanent settlement. Below, the ,,oldest house" has documents to prove it existed as early as 1720. At lower right, a street scene in the restored section known as San Agustin Antiguo.

Here in St. Augustine, where Henry Flagler built his first great hotel, the Ponce de Leon, pride in history affects life in almost every way. Above, Flagler's old hotel has been converted into Flagler College. Next to it, a tourist gets her portrait painted while she sits and waits on the sidewalk. Below right, one of the city's famed horse coaches rests beneath the balcony of an old home. Florida's oldest city is proud of its age.

220

A few years ago, the small Panhandle town of Jay struck oil and the reverberations still have not slowed down. Su

den wealth came to farmers who owned the right land. An oil rush developed in Jay and one result was this refinery.

The timber industry, which owns millions of acres of Florida forests, supplies a series of pulp or paper mills around the state. At left, a plant near Fernandina Beach. At upper right, a logging operation near Perry, which calls itself the tree capital of the world. The picture above at right, the mill that sits along the gulf coast near Port St. Joe. The combination of state and national forests, plus those held in timber, assures north Florida of large areas of greenery. Still, ecologists fear the effect of mill pollution.

These mills turn trees into paper

A blessing for fishing fleet at Destin

An ancient Christian tradition, the blessing of the fishing fleet, here takes place at the Miracle Strip resort and fishing center of Destin. At the service, a fleet of some 90 boats stands off-shore. Each boat passes dockside, where the clergy offer blessings and prayers for a bountiful harvest. Boats which never have been blessed before, must be boarded so that a small wooden cross may be placed near the helm. Destin began the custom in 1958. Since then its commercial, as well as charter boats for sports fishermen, have increased in number considerably. Destin itself – located between Panama City and Fort Walton Beach – has experienced such rapid growth that its beaches now are lined with high-rises.

227

University of Florida: books, bikes, girls, games

In north central Florida, set in an area of lakes, is the University of Florida at Gainesville.
Pines, palms and oaks shade a campus that spreads for miles, making bicycles a handy way to get to class. At left, one student backpacks his books. In the background, an example of the old red brick, Gothic buildings that dominate campus architecture. At right, coeds beat the heat with shorts, and one mindweary lad pillows his head on texts, not the customary way to cram. Below, the university football team, best known as the Fighting Gators, runs through a practice scrimmage. While enrollment and facilities have grown tremendously, the campus charm remains.

A quiet time at sunset, when the sun begins to turn the horizon to red, and fishermen head for home with stories to

tell and the day's harvest to count. A pair of pelicans flap overhead hoping for a few more castoff seafood snacks.

Index

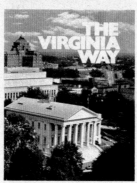
Credit for photographs not taken by Heinz Erhardt:
Al Satterwhite:
pages 70 (1), 83 (2), 107 (1), 108 (1), 130/131 (4).
Flip Schulke:
page 58 (1).
Fred Ward:
pages 59 (1), 132/133 (2).
NASA:
page 160 (1).
Florida Chamber of Commerce:
page 184 (1).
Florida Photo:
page 185 (1).

232